Grass Roots

in Verse

Foreword by James Berry

edited by Arif Ali and Catherine Hogben

HANSIB PUBLISHING

First published in 1988 by Hansib Publishing Limited,
Tower House, 139/149 Fonthill Road,
London N4 3HF, England
Tel: 01-281 1191. Fax: 01-263 9656
Copyright © Hansib Publishing Limited, 1988.

Design, typesetting and production by
Hansib Publishing Limited.

Printed by Hansib Printing Limited,
Unit 19, Caxton Hill Industrial Estate,
Hertford, Herts.
Tel: (0992) 553592

Grass Roots in Verse.
1. Poetry in English, 1945 – Anthologies
I. Ali, Arif II. Hogben, Catherine
821′.914′08

ISBN 1-870518-13-6

Contents

Foreword

The way old habits of fear, animosity, war and barriers-propping operate, they keep old agonies going. Yet – as if we have an underlying, insistent destiny that wants us to develop an empathy with each other, and pool resources continuously – we find that new ways to continue, or start again, do keep cropping up. But for our awareness to widen, and our quality of life improve, the new opportunities have to be recognised, taken up, and used. This anthology demonstrates more than the use of a new opportunity. It underlines belonging, participation, and a vision for development. This means that publishing a book of poems by people in Britain with a Caribbean, Asian and African background is in itself a progressive act.

The cultural background difference between the newcomers to Britain is wide and varied. But it is the similar experience of being black people living here that is commonly highlighted. All in all there is something of how a change of place affects development. And since to express oneself in an art form is to expose private feeling publicly, somewhere in it there will always be a statement about quality of belonging. Significantly, poems here are bound to represent writers who – through all their generations back – for the first time are having their thoughts appear on the printed page.

The quest is for a freer, fuller, social, cultural and economic life. And the people have come to understand that if they are not reflected in poetry, drama, general fiction and the day-to-day radio and TV programmes, it will be understood that everything is already known about them: there is nothing new to be said. Then, perhaps, they don't exist at all. They have come to see that they themselves are the best writers to draw on their source of experience, and they have set about it.

Not surprisingly, much of the work blazes or smoulders with rage, dealing with injustice, frustration, disappointment with background nation, racism and the need to rebel. A general tone of voice comes from 'Journal of a Street Fighter':

> Day 1
> Today I entered the streets of change
> marching;
> with burning hole in my stomach
> and fear gripped tightly in my hand...

Yet – in a kind of celebration – a different confidence observes, relates, assesses. And, like this, a fresh, personal voice records 'The Elephant':

> Elephants were not her cup of tea –
> they were mammoth and boring,
> immobile, they turned no somersaults...
> She avoided those massive tree trunk legs
> and looked straight up at the eyes.
> A storehouse of sorrow was locked in its brain.
> Tentative, she reached out a hand and patted
> the incredible trunk stretched out to her.

Grass Roots in Verse indicates a group of people with a lot to say urgently, and they are in an active state of poetry writing. As a form, to black writers generally, poetry writing is popular. It lends itself to both an absorption and release of strong feelings; it allows public sharing in a reading performance; it has developed popular models with distinctive features which highlight a new confidence of identity through powerful orality. We still have to see if the vigour and style of this new poetry in performance will influence British mainstream poetry presentation.

A new literature is developing in Britain – Black British literature. It is a sensitive response to nurture it and help it emerge to take its place.

James Berry
September 1988

Preface

For many years Hansib Publishing has supplemented the arts pages of its weekly newspapers – *African*, *Asian* and *Caribbean Times* – with regular poetry contributions from its readers. The huge popularity of these features has provided the inspiration for this anthology.

When the idea was proposed, the response was immediate and overwhelming; submissions flooded into the office from all over the country, presenting the editors with the enormous and difficult task of selection. Lacking a precedent for such an anthology, the criterion was not immediately obvious; what was evident, however, and which we have sought to reflect, is the diversity of expression and the enormous range and depth of creative talent resident within the community. The result is a rich assortment, a mixed bag. For this reason, the order of the poems falls alphabetically according to author, rather than thematically or chronologically, lending each an air of unexpectancy, allowing it to reveal itself directly to the reader.

But this is not to suppose that *Grass Roots in Verse* is simply a collection of isolated voices. On the contrary, the poems convey an unmistakable harmony; not only in their shared passion and vigour for the language, but, more significantly, in their resounding urgency to be heard. Each poet speaks from an ancient history of experience, one that demands articulation through a medium that is both immediate and permanent. The subsequent challenge to find and shape a distinctive voice is inextricably bound to the question of language, most especially for those poets for whom the English language is not their first, or for whom it remains a stubborn obstacle to the external processes of cultural assimilation (and one which still infers the equation between dialect and doggerel). Here the challenge has been met head-on. In their path, language has been ambushed, appropriated and made finally to bear the weight of their own experience.

Essentially, *Grass Roots in Verse* is a collection of community verse. It rests upon a belief in the potency of the written word. Furthermore, by its nature, it resists the assumption that poetry is somehow a preserve of an enlightened élite. By usurping such notions of cultural hegemony it offers a simple and, in this month of Carnival, a timely message: that the cultural agenda of any healthy, integrated society must, first and foremost, reflect the sum of all its parts.

Who can speak of your living
Describe your beauty and your grace
Explain that you are crying
When there's laughter on your face.

You have the words and wisdom
The power in your soul
Tell the poem, write the story
Let the words unfold.

Su Andi

Poetry is not for the elite
nor the emotionally discreet.
It's for the mass,
irrespective of their class.
Poetry is fundamental communication,
unimpressed by eloquence
or precise pronunciation.
Once your words are understood
then your prose is good.

Kassmae

F S Abiden
Fareesa Abiden, 17, was born in Karachi, Pakistan, and raised in England. She began writing poetry at 13 and lists as her main influences, "anything and everything... my family and the Doors".

Dear

I locked you up today
didn't I? I'm sorry,
So don't ask me why
I can't tell you.

It was for your sake you see.
Your father came,
only he doesn't know that.
He'd be angry if he found out.
So keep it to yourself
and don't go telling strangers
they'll only talk.
And you would find yourself in the real world
the real, ugly world
that talks and pulls people down.

I didn't mean to tell you this way
and yes, I have a conscience
only it's been pulled and twisted over the years
by your little presence.

As I Drew Near

The floor was dirty, the curtains closed;
I knew you were there.
Uncertain of life, uncertain of everything,
you whinged in a corner, afraid,
as I drew near.

Questions, always questions,
"Why don't you go away?"
you inquired, with red eyes,
I smiled as always,
drawing near.

Your simple thoughts, your simple self,
were never with me; they just screamed.
Enclosed and entangled you gained nothing,
only a guilt ridden conscience
in which I had thrust a spear,
still drawing near.

I left you like death
unmoved, but not at peace.
Still etched in your face,
was the fear of me, and what I could do
by drawing near.

Maureen Adams

Maureen Adams was born in London to Jamaican parents. She currently lives in Wiltshire where she works with the local Social Services Department. Maureen Adams is married with three children.

To Kill With Love

Imagine
Killing a small baby like you
SUCH THOUGHTS!
As I look into your beautiful brown eyes
As I stroke your ebony hair
As I caress your sun-kissed skin

I shake with disgust!

Of course I could not kill you...

But then,
I remembered my ancestor
She faced a terrible dilemma
As she looked into your beautiful brown eyes
As she stroked your ebony hair
As she caressed your sun-kissed skin

Only, in her arms you lay dead.

"But why?" My education asks...

The choice was simple, fool!
To die in purity or live in slavery
And as I remember this
could I kill you, beloved?
                              ... Of course I could.

Pride Child

My name is Carlos
I am Greek
My parents are Greek
My ancestors were Greek, keepers of the Iliad
and its wisdom within.
I am proud of my ancestors

> my parents
> my name
> ...and me.

My people take me seriously.

My name is Sosheel
I am Asian
My parents are Asian
My ancestors were Asian, architects of empires and
travellers through time.
I am proud of my ancestors

> my parents
> my name
> ...and me.

My people take me seriously.

My name is Omo-Delé
My parents are Westindians
My ancestors were Africans, reluctant slaves,
severed from civilisation and survivors of tyranny.
I am proud of my ancestors

> my parents
> my name
> ...and me.

But, my people do *not* take me seriously.
They laugh at my name
They deny my history, and
they are *not* proud of their parents
                                    their ancestors
                                    ...themselves.
They will not survive.

But I will shine like a beacon at sea
For my name is Omo-Delé, and
I am proud that I'm an African and me.

Who Will Carry the Torch Now?

Once, like so many

Immigrants, George Campbell and wife
Dreamed their three sons
Would aspire to be
A doctor, teacher or lawyer.

One generation later
They must be content with
A schizophrenic, a prisoner and a corpse.

So who will 'Carry The Torch'
Now their dream is a nightmare?

Naeem Akhtar Ali
Naeem Akhtar Ali, 17, is a student at East Ham
College, London, preparing for a career in scientific
research.

Elephant Hunter

It sat in front of us like a Buddha,
A huge mountain of flesh,
Towering above the Pygmies,
It's trunk like a slithery self-centred snake.

Our shotguns triggered off piercing screams
All the way into the depths of the jungle.

He rose, meandering,
Dropping like a wall hit by a bulldozer.

A thundering crash echoed like an erupting volcano.

Its skin rippling like a soft breeze over water.

Deborah Akinmoybe
Deborah Akinmoybe, of Nigerian parentage, was born and grew up in Islington, London. She is in her second year of a four year Peace Studies course at the University of Ulster.
The following poem is dedicated to her mother.

Coming Out

"Likewise," said she to her soul...
"Here I am and not a friend to hold."
Deep, deep down she searches
Until cut off from all around.

The quiet anxiety which steals her mind
The unsettled attitudes which develop with time.

"Help!" she cried,
"Let me out soul, I need to be free."

Days once there with time, now appear as tasks
Fought onto the deadening hours
Until everything is quiet.

"Will I make it?" she dares to enquire –
Her fear such that confidence has run.

With a voice so loud, solemn, sincere,
The soul replies
With a menacing glee
"It's up to you (my dear) to set yourself free."

Su Andi
Su Andi is essentially a Performance Poet. Her
previous publications include Poetic License
(Commonword Ltd) and Holding Out *(Crocus*
Books) and her poems have appeared in various
magazines and periodicals. She currently works with
Cultureword, Manchester, as the Black Women
Writers' Development Officer and is a member of
Blackscribe Poets, The Black Arts Alliance and
NAWE. As a black artist, Su Andi is concerned with
"all black (women) art... the struggle is long... long
in coming...but hopefully not far away".

The Black Artist Replies

Written after a workshop in conjunction with the
Manchester City Art Gallery Exhibition 'Hard
Times' when the work produced by black school
girls was seen to be militant by the school deputy
head.

You ask me, to go easy
in re-defining,
your classification.
Unfit to be labelled Human Being.

You ask me
To righten your wrongs.
To heal the wounds opened
by the throngs of your tongues.
The chains of your society,
the corruption of your minds.

You ask me

Ask me nothing.

For I will do as I determine
With all the power of my will.
I will control the pressure of re-education.
And when the true history is told
Who will wear the chip then...?

The Sun

See the sun
See the colours in its rays,
Yellow, orange and gold
Specks of purple.
I see the sun
Yet my eyes are closed.

And the heat
It warms me to my soul
I forget that I have
Ever been cold.

See the sun
    the sun
        summer
        summer.
I saw the sun
    one day
    one summer
    long ago.

Edges Determined by Inner Space

These legs have carried me.
Borne me on.
Through desert plains.
Through jungle wild
With joy sustained
They've carried me.

Across waters wild
To worlds apart
They rested, chained,
To carry me.
Through cotton picked,
Through whip and lash,
Till freedom called
They carried me.

Yet still I shuffle
One inch
One step at a time
To reclaim my space,
Place,
In humanity.

Naseem Anwar

Naseem Anwar, from Karachi, Pakistan, has been writing verse from the age of 15. Recently he has begun to write in his mother tongue – Urdu. Naseem Anwar is a Lecturer with the Racial Equality Unit at Lancashire Polytechnic.

Children of (Sabra and Chatila) Camps

I saw you standing
alone and innocent
already deprived of childhood.
What was your crime?
You were born a Palestinian.
Yet you
did not even know your nationality.
You paid a heavy price
lost all your powers
to speak and hear.
Your tragedy
is my pain.
Your smile,
my tears.
In your eyes
I see the starkness
the question
where were you
when I suffered?
Where was the humanity you all talk about?
I look away
because I know the answer
to which there should not have been a
question in the first place.

What Bicentennial?

The world is celebrating
our enslavement.
It is witnessing an event
marking the rape of our land.
A mass orgy
of destruction and corruption.
Yet it denies
our basic rights
and indulges in self congratulations
of a party
that should never have taken place in history.

New Worlds

Space
Vast
Silent
lies a lonely star
Twinkling
Perhaps it's a signal for the beginning
or the ending
of a world
unknown to mankind.

Saleem Arif
Saleem Hassam Arif, ten, lives in London where he attends Willington school. He lists as his hobbies reading, writing, tennis, photography and playing the piano. In 1987 he received the class prize and a first prize in photography. He has been writing poetry since the age of seven.

Thoughts

The thoughts that rain in their steady glow,
Like stars on life's cold sea,
Which others know, or say they know,
They never shone for me.

Thoughts light, like gleams, my spirits sky
But they will not remain,
They light me once, they hurry by,
And never come again.

Gita Bedi
Gita K Bedi was born in Kenya and came to England as a child. She is a graduate of the University of London and works as a Chartered Librarian.

'Ere She Said

'Ere she said,
Her fag hanging out of her mouth,
Dropping both ash and H's.
'Ere she said,
Was you born 'ere?
Only you speak very good English
Where d'ya come from then?
Africa?

Only askin' 'cos what's 'er name come from there
But she ain't your colouring,
She's darker, much darker
Than you.

And do ya eat food – like what we do?
Y'know, red meat and Yorkshire Pud?
Only what's 'er name says she don't.
She eats – what d'ya call 'em –
Balls of dough, fried like dumplings.

'Ere she said. Listen to this.
I've bin wif out 'eat for five weeks,
Just bin onto the Council.
But the man said he couldn't unnerstan' me.
Didn't unnerstan' me accent.
Bleeding Asian weren't he.

Sorry... din't mean you.
I mean you're not like the rest of 'em.
Are you?

Zydah Benjimin
Zydah Benjimin was born in England in 1962 and works in the community, specialising in infant child care. She enjoys travelling and considers it an important stimulus for her writing.

Footprints in the Sand

Time passes by
As we cross this land
And now I'm looking back
To see my footprints
In the sand.
In some places
There are spaces
And no footprints do I see,
But you've shown me
That when I most needed you
It was then
You carried me

Rastafari

A So it Go

A so it go you know.
Money scarce
Times getting worse
But you still have to hope
No time to sit around and mope
A so it go you know.
Raising children
Who want to be unruly
Tending to them
Or the house – or men
As if it was your duty,
No time to know yourself
Be yourself or
Really feel yourself.
A so it go you know, Sista
For now.

Just Like a Candle

Father and mother gave you life
Into the world you came,
Just like a candle you must light it to give it a flame.
And as the years go on, with each day Jah sends,
Just like a candle burning slowly to the end.
Life's so unreliable,
Danger could be anywhere about,
Just like a candle, a quick draught will blow it out.
And as time keeps moving,
And tiredness fills your eyes,
Just like a candle starts to flicker and then dies.

Rifa Bhunnoo
Rifa Bhunnoo is of Mauritian origin and is presently living in south London. As well as belonging to a writers' workshop, Rifa Bhunnoo is a regular contributor to her school magazine, and the magazine Shocking Pink 11. In 1987 she won the Dillons Young Reader Competition.

A Chance

She doesn't understand much
Of what is going on around her
But she feels it.
She can't kiss or hug or cry
But she can love you.
She doesn't always notice if you're there
Or not
But she wants you.
Just don't ignore her.
There's more to her than meets
The eye.

Underneath this exterior,
Which makes you uncomfortable
And callous,
Is a world
Full of imagination, ideas,
And creations.
She's not stupid.
She's special.
Just give this girl
A Chance.

Busker

I stand and study the people
Walking, bustling along

I am the Watcher.

They don't know I am here;
They don't realise
That my whole life
Depends on those pennies
Scattered in my case.
They don't listen
To the music
Echoing around the
Chambers of the Underground –
I'm an insignificant
Speck of dust
My music a backdrop to
Their empty lives
This music is my life

I survive.

Richard Harry Binks
Richard H Binks, 20, was born in Batley, West
Yorkshire, and is studying at Leeds Polytechnic for a
diploma in Applied Biology. His poetry is largely
influenced by the landscape of the Yorkshire
countryside, where he has lived all his life. Richard
Binks, whose interests include jazz, classical
literature and opera, hopes to publish his first volume
of verse in 1989.

Gordale Scar

Minnow shoals
Of sideways floating
Drops – they stun
And tease
And beckon
To come close!

Obedient, I descend
Some awkward, slippery
Stones – clinging to
Whatever the panicking hand
Chances to meet – feeling
The finger's softness left
On bruising rock...

The canyon deftly unrolls
Its intricacies – a new perspective
At each fumbling step.

Once more the sun
Comes out – once more
They scintillate, bouyant,
A cloud of sequinned
Butterflies gleamed from

The rock-face – a unison
Of silver lightness...

My eyes lashes net to catch
That moisture – also, the curling
Lip and savouring tongue –
Gently it comes to rest
On flushed and upturned cheeks...

I've walked long,
But this – so suddenly revealed
Is more than surprising boon;
In this I am one – a hard, eager
Fist closing around eager beauty's
Kernel – mine!

Minnow shoals
Sideways carried
Through the air – behind,
The looming, sweat pouring
Sculpture of dark rock.

Solitude

Oh. It's fine when you live alone,
In a cottage away on the distant hills,
To bustle with crowds in the teeming town
And let their chattering gossip
Fill your soul with pleasure at being a man.
Laughing and joking with a pint of ale.
But it palls, it palls and again the span
Of the far horizon beckons and calls,
And the way of solitude, no-one in sight,
Shared with curlew and rock-hanging falls –
You are more than a man at the dawn of light
You are part of the universe, through and through.
You are one of its units daily renewed,
A cloud wind-blown sailing the blue.

Wayne B Carr
Wayne B Carr teaches English to ethnic minority
children in Hillingdon. He is married and he and his
wife have one daughter.

Britannia Visited

1899

Suzerainty marked in red on the classroom map
which charts the far-flung caboodle.
From Pacific reef to snowed-on pine
a vast freebootin' enterprise born
from uncertain starts, strung together by boots,
barrels, swaggers, ships of the line and its motley
natives steaming from Port Stanley to Rangoon,
alike in tutelage to a God-given right to rule.

Now memsahibs play quoits on poop decks,
while Sahibs take char served from verhandas
by houseboys with walk-on parts; whiskered lips
stiffened by cold baths at public school
droop in the torrid haze of this late afternoon;
tiresome rumours drift upwards from the teeming
plains far below the lodge of Simla
where the viceroy fumes then sighs; meantime
soldiers of the Queen blunder uphill to Spion Kop
while, slightly beyond the frame,
under burning skies, Lord Kitchener's volunteers
are trundling over the top.

1919

I

Amritsar and dawn breaking,
The sun, red as a wound,
beginning to volley off its full bore heat.
The town breaks into sweat
washing from pilgrims' pores in water troughs that
usher in the temple ground
lapped by a blue lake surround,
before immersion in the cool
of golden dome and marble colonnade.
Now the heat strikes the building tops,
sights a rabid dog lurching, mad enough to shun
the awning's shade and, raising its blood-crazed eye,
stares into the muzzle of the sun,
into a raging sky.

II

Swarming in this maggot heat
flames snarl, snap, leap to gulp down the schools,
churches, the Town Hall, leaving shells strewn and
blistered black.
Cries for 'white blood'
slash through the smoke,
through telegraph wires dangling
like demented spiders' webs
dog Mr Stewart who, clubbed senseless,
burns, his bank a charred mangle,
hound Miss Sherwood who, howled from her bike,
is lacerated blue.
What is it breeds this blood?
Leaders' arrests? Stones called by shots?
Change craved by pale lives?
Whatever, the mob foams for it,
draws it by the minute till the whole town runs for
blood or safety.

Exhausted calm resonates
the soldiers' boots to thunder
as they wind the sullen streets
grinding martial law,
trampling public meetings,
By Order, R E H Dyer,
General Officer Commanding.

III

Why this fixed look,
General,
this temple-throbbing anger
towards evening on the day?
News just in confirms reports
of a law-defying meeting in the Jallianwala Bagh.
Do old injuries under horse,
old heat stroke and malaria
fire your grizzled frame,
or is it that lady's violated
honour strikes you to a flame?
Meanwhile the charge smoulders in your gun,
is carried by heavy-lidded eyes
too much in the sun,
eyes that see only black and white,
the Raj without question is right.
Even if we would we cannot
stop you now General;
the heat's ordained, the elements cocked,
pointing at this hour,
drawing you with his fifty rifles
towards History, towards the Garden
forever grafted to your name.

IV

Eight acres in parch brown,
the Bagh. Despite its name,
no flowers, no lawns, no shade
to wallow a buffalo's hide;

on one side a well,
the lot penned by walls.
Inside the huge crowd sits, sleeps, sprawls,
half hearing speeches,
then pound, pound, distempered feet,
soldiers suddenly, a line bristling.
Seconds suspend each life as time crawls, stops
dead.
The General, cap down over eyes,
barks 'Fire! Rapid Fire!'
'They've had their warning,' he said.
Sarees ruffle in disbelief, a baby cries,
panic screams, bullets knive,
rain like stones on a mad cur,
welling, sluicing as barrels train
where the crowd is thickest, flailing bodies
that choke the exit's narrow alleyways,
while into piles spent shells fall,
settle, till backs stiffen,
march off into distance.

V

Blood and barrels cold,
the soldiers have marched into the dark,
their lesson, hammered to the walls,
denied by forces louder than guns,
stronger, finer than the
unbending will which abandoned
the victims
to the curfewed night.
Creeping, pale daylight lingers,
picking details clean,
the blood splashed well,
the torsoes heaped,
twisted by the walls,
the turbans lopped and scattered
on the ground,

while the days intervene,
laying the great distended scream,
bringing to that reeking blood,
the garlanded sweetness of the
funeral pyre's sandalwood,
fading the General whose spleen
was vented making the natives crawl
like beasts in atonement on all fours.
In their place the ghostly bullets play
across the tender and green
from flowering shrubs, cypress
trees, tended lawns and hedges.
May the shade cool hot blood
and jasmine with its white lighten
this burden peace.

1947

Carried away by wars, fevers and
splendours past,
from Madras, Simla to Bangalore
the Empire's own
crumble beneath effigies in
weeping stone,
stiff upper lips grinning at last
far away from home. Indifferent to these,
file mounts on dusty file faded, unread,
the Ganges sweeps on ashen with her dead,
squalor and famine cry out on
beggared knees.

A matchstick man in dhoti against
the viceroy's throne
has pitched an ashram,
satyagraha, a spinning wheel.
Midnight looms, the tryst when

freedom will awake.
Sundering the gloom, the foul-
faced furies hone,
a passion no waters wet or fasts can heal,
willing his rare-spun thread to break.

You

When you were small as a button
and big as a new world,
like settlers at dawn we came,
Daddy's side Caucasian,
Mummy's side Asian,
seeking familiar marks,
each one staking a claim.
Your fine light hair, now curled,
was claimed by Gran
on behalf of Dad,
both believing your skin was white
(well, pink really),
not that we intended any slight
to Mum whose skin was brown
so not like yours, clearly.

But now the stakes were down;
your visitors' amble
rapidly turned an African scramble.
Grandad Brown said you're like Grandma White
who threw her arms in disbelief,
then started disclaiming all in sight.
Surely it was more than plain
to anyone who knows
that you took their side
from your shape of head and toes
and what about your nose!
The Browns assured themselves
her glasses lied
it was her jaundice
that she spied.

Dad struck another note
and saw you for a singer
from the start;

when your midnight wails
played major-minor scales
which drummed across his heart,
he vowed such passion should be neutered
by being finely tutored
so tuned you to the music of Mozart.
Mum had you on another track,
bending Newton's laws
by vaulting and leaping
through the great outdoors.
We should have known better.

Narcissus-like we roved your pools,
saw ourselves reflected there,
with us thereby the greater fools;
for you of course are you,
a shade between Mum, Dad
and all the others. Besides,
whether of eye or limb,
you have no end that we can see,
for edging you is something dim
or nimbus-like,
dwarfing those who shove
out your bark
through the dark
on a rising tide of imperfect love.

Nirmal Chandra Deb
Nirmal Chandra Deb was born in India in 1942, and educated in East Pakistan where he worked as an Assistant Headmaster before taking the post of Clerk in the civil court. He currently lives and works in London where he is a Catering Manager. His poems have appeared in various Bengali and English newspapers.

I Need You

I need you.
Need you to share
My good times;
Share my bad times.

I need you.
Need you to give
Me company
Whenever
I feel lonely.

I need you.
Need you to give
Me inspiration when
I am depressed.

I need you.
Need you to charm
Me whenever I
Am sad and
miserable.

I need you.
Need you at my
Side; without you
I feel poor at heart.

Do Not Cry My Boy

Do not cry, my boy.
Do not cry, cry not.
If you cry so, so you
will cry your whole life.

Do not cry, my boy.
Cry not for your failure.
Failures will bring you success.

Do not cry, my boy.
If you cry so, so you
make your life miserable.
Life is for struggle, you
remember so.

Do not cry, my boy.
Repent not for setbacks,
or you will live on
self pity.
Laugh off any of your hard feelings
and let your mind be
free.

Do not cry, my boy.
Be brave in life.
Let your heart be strong
in painful situations.
Ignore the misdeeds
of the mischievous.

Cry not, my boy, do not cry.
Take life easy and be happy, go lucky.
Keep patience and thus get on
with life.
Be firm and persevering.

So, do not cry, my boy.
Enjoy the nectar of nature, look
at the funny side of
life and cry no more.

Kenneth Charles
Kenneth Charles was born in the Westindies and now
lives in Huddersfield. His poetry is concerned with
the power struggle black people face worldwide.

Restless Sands of Time

Lonely dancer across the floor
Twisting, turning, dancing, to and fro
Like a dancer I knew before.
Shadows in front of the fire glow
Under the night sky so long ago.

The outline of her body stood out profoundly
Virginal, untouched,
Sweet nakedness clothed in jewelled array
Gold, rubies, diamonds, pearls.

In a country my eyes had never seen
Feelings though as if my feet had been
Lands abound with plentiful
Its people free and beautiful
Many come to watch the dancer
Punching bibles, selling beads
Stepped ashore in all their glory
Merchant men or were they thieves?

Now a widow this barren land
Stripped bare of wealth
Raped, defiled, the dancer –
Tentacles of the western world.

Dr Debjani Chatterjee
Debjani Chatterjee was born in Delhi and won the
Shankar's International Children's Prize for poetry
in her teens. She is currently employed by the
Sheffield Council for Racial Equality.

Tagore

Bengal and all the world have drowned you,
Tagore, in great respect, but there is
No yearly resurrection. Garlands
Of saturation songs have sickened
The same society which wore you
Romantic on its sleeve, now withered.
But waves of time will wash these strangers.
Immortal words on sand are carried
By sea, and hang from skies grown weary.
But tidal waves recede now clawing
Salt marks that stroke your face. Though fashion
Decries you, artist, poet, songster,
The critics live by rules – obscurely.
No matter what, you saw the beauty
That lights the dark girl's deep eyed lustre.
You smiled in prayer, moved in worship,
You sang in language, loving, earthy.
No matter what, one reads enchantment
In words, like bamboo piercing city
Pollution: struggling, breathing, haunting.

All the Arts

The strings of life twang and resonate,
A mournful shahnai moans and trembles.
Does this music jar on ears
Finely tuned to an orchestrated past?
It is our interface that is discordant.
Where is the harmony of souls in unison?

All dance is struggle, swirling, whirling,
Beating on the consciousness.
Arts that haunt the empty galleries,
Pattering on the eardrums in tongues
That are calls of silent minorities.
Sustaining selfhood, creating space,
Providing an oppositional culture
To framework the vision of resistance
That demands a stage, where music reverberates
Till it threads an echo in hollow halls
Hallowed by "traditional culture".
High art, low art, art for art, community art...

All movement is political expression,
The art of creative hunger-pains that protest
At the parched aridness of unawareness.
Many voices that raise a righteous anger,
Share a perception, an outstretched hand,
To communicate friendship, to celebrate,
An invitation to explore a vision,
A triumphant call to liberation,
To understand where progress lies, and finally
To embrace all the arts as affirmation.

(This poem was first published in *The Black Arts Day* Report by Sheffield Council for Racial Equality & Sheffield Arts Department in January 1987.)

Reflection

Grandparents sit with children,
still, for once, on their knees,
all smiling, all smart,
in the sunshine garden.
Captured for posterity
is all that family togetherness,
the sense that we go on forever.
My shy cousin leaning her plaited head
on the grand wicker armchair,
is married now to a business tycoon.
The spoilt little one looks up
from kohl fringed eyes
and shows off his fire engine painted red
and unique in the neighbourhood
for its strident sound.
My sensible brother stands at the edge
but still manages to give the impression
that he is shepherding us children in.
My sister's expression of concentration
is the same one I often see
on my nephew doing homework.
There's a faint look of anxious-to-get-away
and I remember all the adventures
of that garden just beyond the picture frame:
the crocodile and bank game we played,
especially hilarious in monsoon weather;
the temple worship for which we gathered
flowers, leaves and stones,
taking it in turn to be head priest,
and how carefully we observed the rule
about removing our sandals and canvas shoes;
we played at patriots too and drove out the British
again and again...
My grandfather is sitting ramrod straight,

the head of the house, a self-made man
with a title from the Raj for services
rendered, a war-time Ministry of Defence.
His patrician nose on a stern brown face
belies the warm and gentle eyes.
My grandmother sports the largest red dot
on her forehead and her round face
beams her pleasure, her gusto in life.
A red bordered white sari drapes her head,
a handsome woman, full of strength.
I am standing self-conscious
and holding up the lacy new frock
so that the knickers peep at the camera.
Somewhere in the middle of the picture
I am posing and doing my duty.

The Elephant

Elephants were not her cup of tea –
they were mammoth and boring,
immobile, they turned no somersaults.
Gaiety and the antics of monkeys
and insulting parakeets,
blinking and chattering,
offered her the warmth of fur and vivid feathers.
Elephants were distinct, tusked and ominous.
Powerful and towering over children,
their long memories and wisdom
placed them in a different zoo for adults.
"But this is an Indian elephant,"
her father said. "It is homesick
and will cheer up to see an Indian girl
in this wet, cold, foreign land."
So she tore away from the noisy cages
and allowed herself to be slowly led
to greet her majestic compatriot.
She avoided those massive tree trunk legs
and looked straight up at the eyes.
A storehouse of sorrow was locked in its brain.
Tentative, she reached out a hand and patted
the incredible trunk stretched out to her.

Abdullahi D Dan-Asabe
Abdullahi D Dan-Asabe was born in Nigeria and
now lives and works in London. His poems have
previously appeared in a number of Nigerian
journals.

The Heritage

Have patience sleeping memoriams
If your name is buried with you
For the market you left
Is still crowded
Flourishing with those same goods you knew
Till it closes for the day
Your children would stay

Forgive them sleeping memoriams
If you were arraigned before colourful faces
Soundy gongs and melodious choir
Wine infested mourners and pipe addicts
For they invoke your living spirit
As they distort your unspoken wants

And to the dry lands
Where silence threatens your loneliness
With scenty chaplets and distant cries
That remind you of missing obligations

Drowned are your children in the crowd
Wearing faces of archaic bereavement
With a hereditary blood of neglect
And a mystic mind
Like those flourishing goods

Sleep so consoled memoriams
The children are good
They have inherited your wisdom
To bid you farewell

E Gordon De'Cage

E Gordon De'Cage was born in Jamaica in 1955, and educated in England. He works as an Advertising Salesman, and his interests include vedic philosophy, psychology, writing and yoga. A number of his poems were recently published in a North American poetry anthology.

Ketchup

An' yu pop shit
An' cuss bad wud
An' yu gwan like yu's a fool
An'yu play de skank
An'yu tink yu smart
An'yu say yu na get cart
But ya gwan – gallang de...
Yu soon get yu ketchup, ketchup!

Unsettled Whisperings

Leaning on a shadow,
It looks like midnight in your dreams
When macabre phantoms stretch the imagination
And penniless thought-slaves work overtime.
Feel the mind climbing stealthily
Out of shape,
Then let the gibbering monkey clamour senselessly
On the make;
And watch the overheated oven of your life
Spoil your beautiful little cake.

Make him the Grand Master of his life
For a meagre day;
Now hear the unsettled whisperings of weird things
He's got to say.
The spinning ball never hurts the cricket bat
But the indentations of memory live on,
And certain is the painful tension
Of the tight boot you force on
When the love of all love is thrown
Violently out of joint.

An' de Monkey's on Yu Back

An' de monkey's on yu back,
An' him-a-hack, an' him-a-hack.
An' de monkey's on yu back,
An' de bull-whip in yu back, him sah yu too slack.
An' de monkey's on yu back,
An' Ma'sa sah yu's a bease-a-burden,
good fi nutton.
An' de monkey's on yu back,
But dis ya arse stub'orn yu kno'!
An' de monkey's on yu back,
An' him-a-get an' him-a-get rich an' fat.

An' de monkey's on yu back,
An' him a feed dis dawg a rotten piece a scat.
An' de monkey's on yu back,
An' him-a-rape an'pillage – just like dat.
An' de monkey's on yu back,
But wait!
Disya carrot in fronta me nose taise like plastic.
An' de monkey's on yu back,
An' Bwoy! Him jus gimme de crocus-bag-sack.
An' de monkey's on yu back,
An' tell me what chance yu 'ave wen yu lack.
An' de monkey's on yu back,
An' him ridin' high an'screwin' like a vampire bat.

An' de monkey's on yu back,
An' him na let up yu kno' – dats a fack.
An' de monkey's on yu back,
An' him say broder, yu 'aven't got de knack.
An' de monkey's on yu back,
An' Tunda an'lightnin' comin' dung, an' yu soakin'
wet.

An' de monkey's on yu back,
An' him-a-wear a pink cravat an' look like a sap.
An' de monkey's on yu back,
An' him-a-fuck, an' him-a-fuck.
An' him-a...Ch'a...Fuck me up.

Perminder Dhillon-Kashyap
Perminder Dhillon-Kashyap was born in Kenya and educated in Kenya and Britain. She works as a freelance Writer, Video Producer, and Media Training Consultant, as well as studying part time for an M A. Her extensive voluntary commitments take her to India every year.

The Inspired Me

To be free from the reigns
of my conscious mind –
conditioned, directed, attuned
to the unnatural.

To be free from the constraints,
the moulds and the holds
of others
and of mine.
To reach the peaks of oblivious
inspiration,
to stoop to the core of pain
and love.

To really live in the body,
the mind,
and the soul.

To be tested on the threshing floor
of knowledge.
To mingle with the love divine,
forgetful, forgotten.

To surface in the universal spirit,
To be, to become, to see.

That would be me...
Becoming me.

Patrick Duffy
Patrick Duffy was born in Kingston, Jamaica in
1951. After winning a COHSE Trades Union
Scholarship to Ruskin College, Oxford, he did post-
graduate work at Oxford Polytechnic before taking
up his present position as Business Lecturer and
Psychotherapist. Patrick Duffy is the founder
member of the Nurses Defence Committee and editor
of Message from a Starship.

She Was Already Falling

She dreamt she was a princess,
Had slain the dragon,
Now was laying on her side,
By some prince charming,
With a silver dagger and a smile,
But before this, she was already falling.

When they lay her down to sleep,
The sky was very black, rain was falling,
People were shuffling,
Someone was coughing,
An individual crying for us dying,
But before this, she was already falling.

When they lay her down to sleep,
She was weak,
Hands so strong that cradled many babies,
Were straining to unlock the door,
Guard against the voices calling,
But before this, she was already falling.

245 T

Went for a walk, what did I see?
I saw a kite strike the sky. That was yesterday.
Today the clouds are not moving.

A car roars into the distance,
An old woman stooping.
A chain of children stooping,
A chain of children running,
A clock across the road striking,
Hardly hear your own breathing on this street.

Went for a walk, what did I see?
People in a shop full of consumers.
Crushed but not touching unless in the mind.
Talking but not hearing.
Pushing money across a counter,
Outdoing the Joneses, Smiths, Murphys and Singhs,
Vomiting at their purchases.

Went for a walk, what did I see?
Out of the city, out of the reach of its heavy metals,
The rain which tastes of sulphur.
I began to feel kind of free.
Touching totality with TM and skipping across
        infinity by pm.
Fully integrated and no longer regressing in tune
        with the cosmos,
I watched the crops being sprayed, the birds
        were singing.
And the weeds welcomed the fall of 245 T.

"This bird's wings are broken..."

This bird's wings are broken,
Yet it sings of the bright lights,
It's sighs are skyward.

This bird's wings are broken,
It trembles in the morning,
Lies hidden from the sharp eyes.
This bird's wings are broken.
It no longer rides the sun,
The stars are deaf, no longer linger on its song.

"I walk along the beach with you..."

I walk along the beach with you,
We enter a thousand cafes and there is always room.
You fill the senses with your perfume,
We drink hot coffee slowly and the tide is in.
From where we sit the sky and sea are blue,
Fishermen talk to you of the past,
Only you are looking at me.

This finger, this foot, this leg were lost at sea,
They spin across a universe
Sharing the fate of those gone on,
We hang on by fingertips
To tales of gales and girls made from elastic,
Fights and sleepless nights and willing mermaids.
Fishermen talk to you, only you are looking at me.

We share thoughts that were dreams of old men.
From the sound of your heart,
You are missing at sea.
Shall we strain every nerve by the hour for a
sighting?
Dark exciting cafes, touched by a strand of lighting.
Fishermen talk to you, only you are looking at me.

Avril Evans
Avril Evans, 19, has been writing poems and short stories since she left school, and is working towards being a full time writer.

The Reconciliation

In the beginning,
I was frail and pure,
Now I want to forgive you,
Once and for all.

You looked smaller,
Looking out onto the horizon,
A thin pale figure,
Where have all the years gone?

When I was younger,
I would come here to escape
From all the pressures of life,
To this desolate place.

I was resentful and full of hatred
When I found out you were here,
Tell me your side of the story,
The one I did not hear.

Memories fill my head,
We were together for many years
Before he came along
And changed all my ideas.

Amos Ford
Amos Ford was born in Belize. He came to Britain in
1941 on secondment to the Ministry of Supply,
Forestry Division, to do war work. Currently retired
from the civil service, but occupied full-time as a
writer, Amos Ford has published extensively on
Caribbean history.

In Memory of My Mother 1885-1975

When young I did tarry at the start,
At the taverns where great men frequent.
I listened and learnt the truth about the heart.
Why hesitate, why tarry and then depart?

What makes men wise but yet hesitant,
Did imagination guide their weary footsteps?
Or did nature ordain that they be constant?
MOVE, move but slowly, while the Angels sleep!

So listen to your heart as she in silence speaks
Your deepest thoughts and assures immortal soul
That love makes no demands upon the weak,
But assures the strong that love is the centre of the
Soul!

Why then deny the heart its consciousness?
When to love is nature's great and noble gift.
To those who seek her in happiness,
now's the time, hurry for she soon departs!

Silently I sit and watch the clouds slip by,
I wonder what message they carry?
For the soul they meet on high
Though not for me the bliss for them to tarry!

Here below or up in the sky, to thee devoted shall I
     be.
Sweet caress, it is for thee I live or die,
But moments not to forget, so shall I say of thee
For you and you alone, I live. Be it so even in the
Sky!

And so believe you me, no other soul but yours
Can sooth and calm my anguished heart,
As I sit and languish for you that cares
Wondering about the workings of the human heart.

My heart is full to overflowing
With devotion for someone not too far from me,
Do spirits ever carry the message or the knowing?
If so say it was you who set me free.

Steve Garner
Steve Garner was born in 1963. Originally from Norwich, he now lives in Oxford and is a post-graduate student at Warwick University, Centre for Caribbean Studies.

Uneconomic Poet

Due to cutbacks in expenditure
imposed by the Ministry of Brevity
this poem will henceforth be
administered by civil servants
whose task it will be to:

i) shorten
ii) curtail
iii) abridge
iv) abbreviate
v) reduce
vi) contract
vii) compress
viii) scrimp
ix) skimp
x) boil down
xi) retrench
xii) cut short
xiii) pare down
xiv) whittle down
xv) clip
xvi) dock
xvii) lop
xviii) prune
xix) crop
xx) bob
xxi) truncate
xxii) hew

and xxiii) foreshorten
the aforesaid poem.
Thereby saving taxpayers money
by rendering the poem
cost-effective and
economically viable.

Only one poet will lose his job.

The Decline and Fall of the Rhyming Umpire

Shouting slaps the drunken moment's cheek
And tension grinds its raucous teeth.
The umpire crouches – wise as Zeus
Gauging good and evil's sullen truce.
A spool of recollections turns beneath
The panama hat. Hinges of experience creak.

On days as these, sun-sodden, endless,
He'd spent the summers of his life
Strumming rural rhythms slow
And steady, downing beer by the glow
Of August evenings. Met his wife
Here after the war. Their futures boundless.

Brought the boy to the clubhouse most weekends.
He kept score, teasing dad but proud, wide-eyed
When his luck was in. Sought his youthful
Face in old school team photos full
Of the doomed and serious young who died
Men's deaths in boys bodies. Absent friends.

He measured time by the shrinking debt
Between skills of father and son.
Passed on tales of combat and the ancient world;
Bradman, Baldwin, the flag unfurled at
    El Alamein
Street parties when the war was won.
Not just another place, another planet.

Now the overs left to him are few.
He plays out his last balls in fading light
With a dead bat in September's cool.
Alone. His partners accepted the cruel

Logic of dismissal. Just one night
In Tunis claimed three in curfew.

The fulcrum of justice, his finger
Raised, as Romans dipped their thumbs
At gladiators.
Guilty or not we all must go when the umpire says
In life's scorebook there are no
"Not Outs" at the end of play. The crumbs
Of teatime swept away and no excuse to linger.

"Please Don't Feed the Poetry"

It's a guarded secret. Or it soon will be.
Poetry as still-life, relic, fossil.
Editors charge the masses fifty p.
to gaze in awe at poems. Aloof and still.
"LOOK BUT DON'T TOUCH". Armed police
supervise the queue. These chosen scribes are dined
by Ministry men in the peace of Whitehall rooms.
Bursaries and beaujolais their bribes.

Beyond museums of frozen, sponsored art
a language evolves. Its guttural cries
honed on determination to tear apart
the veils that bind the poets' eyes –
Self-inflicted bandages. "See-No-Evil" writers
distort the people's sight by omission.
They leave mere stuggle to the fighters
and review the Index of the New Inquisition.

Officials on the marble balcony
watch the milling subjects collect
their cultural rations.
"PLEASE DON'T FEED THE POETRY"
they may as well say, or "Show some respect
for the dead". One woman's coat hides
her "food" that eluded security.
She smashes cases fast before the guides
reach her. Silence is the prelude to articulacy.

Norfolk 'n' Good

"Very flat, Norfolk." Noel Coward.

Those who curl their lip and deem you "flat"
don't know you. There are things more beautiful
than hills, and other ways of expressing their
absence. Becoming your lover is a patient game,
full of subtle revelations;
the quality of evening light caressing a field of corn,
a silence between North Sea waves,
a set of wooded curves reveal
a perfect Saxon church I'd never seen.

An only child city, veined with pubs
and churches – a place for drunken sinners.
One step removed here.
Not behind the times, astride them.
On this spot, Kett's men, for beginners,
disengaged one Earl from his fortune's wheel.
Bishops, cobblers, merchants, Lollards sent for
burning. Lifetimes ago this was a more
influential place but she's grown old
gracefully and still courts younger men.
Wrinkles wear well on her face.

So explain again how flat my county is.
As if it's a can of beer left open too long,
a punctured tyre on a disused bike,
or the wrong note sung in your favourite song.
"Flat is as flat sees" I'd say to that.
The accent gently undulates, the sea
looms loud as mountains, the past towers above.
These are contours which satisfy me.

Monsters

Exist?
Dragons may not,
but monsters do!
Like Hydras,
for every one caught
seven more take its place.

Hunting along society's cracks,
leaving valium shockwaves
amongst grieving relatives,
those held dear.

You can follow their tracks
in the papers.
Their victims strewn across the news.

Believe in them?
You may not,
perhaps.

Yet if you have ever started
at footsteps in a streetlamp's shadow.
Wondered,
one night
with slight trepidation,
what hides behind the face of a stranger?

Then,
their breath has soiled you.
Belief or not.
Tainting your life.

One night,
you too could meet a monster,
feel its bloody paws.

Milton Godfrey
Milton Godfrey was born and educated in Jamaica.
He arrived in England in the early 1960s and worked
variously as a soldier in the British Army, a Singer,
Salesman and Music and Creative Writing Tutor,
before obtaining a BA degree in 1980. Formerly a
Freelance Journalist, Milton Godfrey continues to
write plays, short stories and poems. He also writes,
directs and performs for the theatre and is Co-
ordinator of the Handsworth Community Theatre.

Disappointment

He boarded the plane
In innocence;
Imagined a reality,
But was disappointed
Within hours.
No gold-paved streets
Or welcome that excites,
Just smoke filled atmosphere
From a bird's eye view,
And on landing, a plot
That thickens.

He is not innocent anymore,
Neither can he save the
Return fare.

Inside Looking Out

The sky is grey
It's cold outside.
Windows rattle,
Breezes penetrate
Every crevice.
Curtains flutter
And sway.

While raindrops
Beat out rooftop rhythms,
Smoke from chimneys twirl
Forming images that quickly
Disappear in the drizzle,
And dampness create mists that
Slowly drift.

Wet asphalt and dirty pools
Reflect distorted images
On empty streets.

Suspicion

A Bible story was told
To be
Of love and peace
And joy
That people cared
And how they love
But I think it's
Just a ploy.

The teacher doesn't
Like my hair
The children think
I'm a pain
My mother she says
Never mind
And I try never
to complain.

And people aren't
Too friendly
I can tell the way
They look at me
But I don't really care
At all
Cause I feel brave
And free.

My Sunday best is
Useless now
My shoes are almost worn
And father says there's
No work
The factories are all
Closed down.

The police aren't too kind
To me
They think that I'm
Non plus
And everytime they
Search me
They tell me it's for sus.

Sometimes I think that
Life's not fair
Sometimes I ponder when,
I often wonder what
Will happen
When I reach the age
Of ten.

Alison Graham
Alison Graham, born in County Durham, lives and works as a Teacher in the West Midlands. She describes herself as a "story teller" and hopes to see her short stories published in the near future.

In Their True Colours

Happy Birthday, children!
Oh, thank you, Granny.
Look, Mumma, mine's about Daniel in the lions'
den. And mine's about Joseph in the land of Egypt.
What lovely books they are!
You are lucky, children.

Who did the illustrations?
Who are the publishers?
At last they are showing
The people of Egypt and the children of Israel
In their true colours,
Not white, but black.

Granny's blue eyes twinkle
And she gives a little sigh,
I see the brown felt tips lying on the table.
I did all except the covers
She explains in a murmur,
The surface is too glossy.
I look again and see the pink faces on the covers.

Thank you, Mum, you're marvellous
I whisper humbly.
I put my arm around her
In love and gratitude,
I kiss her stiff fingers

With respect and admiration
For her willingness to change
Her view of the world,
And to see life afresh
Through the eyes of my children.

Themba Greene
Themba Greene was born and raised in Birmingham.
A Rastafarian, he is currently living and working
with homeless people in London.

Just an Illusion

No feel a feeling like this before
This loving sensation new to me
May only last a night
But dear to me it will be in my memory

Hear today, gone tomorrow

Wondering what it's all about
Was it right or terribly wrong
I don't know
For the feeling as gone

Hell, who cares, it was me and you
All considerations and principles
Out the door
For now I'm living
For now I'm learning

Hear today, gone tomorrow

If I had my way
I'd run away, run away
Run but my shadow won't go
Away

Last Penny

Ah right...hush...
come on, hush now...
COME ON, get up!
Stop de the ball-ing inna de middle of de place.
De train full a people an you a rave an a shout
an a ball...wah wrong with you?

O...you have problems...
we all have problems me dear,
come, wipe your mouth and get offa de floor.
Yea, that's right...straighten up yourself.

Me know times rough
but try an control yourself,
know yourself, control yourself,
don't be drag down by the whirlpool...fight.
Control yourself...come offa de ground.

Yea, you alright now?
Good.
Yea, bye, bye now.

Look deh to rah-ted.
An I taught I was on my last penny.

Faith

Lying, still on my back
thinking of myself
as the only being in Existence.
Lying, still on my back
working over small foolish things
and feeling sorry.

I awoke from my negative dream
aware of a Silence
of life and power
a Silence of faith and hope
a Silence of righteousness and peace.
This becoming of awareness
sparked a fire of happiness
where all self-ignorance
is consumed.

So have faith in that power
which rides upon the Silence.

Lying, still on my back
I give thanks
and praise.

Cleveland Hamilton
Cleveland Hamilton is a lawyer from Georgetown,
Guyana.

Guyana

Hold your hand
Soldier
Cop
Stand at ease
let the people congregate
like the stars of the firmament
and the light shine
on the speakers words
about freedom

Hold your hand
Soldier
Cop
Who told you to shoot
the silent crowds
listening to the thunder of the revolution

Take your hand
off the trigger
Soldier
Cop
Let the blood of the youth
bubble and boil
while they call the liberation
down from the horizon

Don't be a fool
Soldier
Cop
Flick on the safety catch

put that gun down
who are you going to shoot?
The weary women in long, tedious queues?
Your mothers
the nine month burden bearers
whose bellies burned for you?
Your grandmothers
who cut your navel strings?

Who you going to shoot
Cop, Soldier
Your brothers
flushing in the anger of
your own veins?
Your sisters
blooming and beautiful?
Your women who sleep with you
and bear your sons and daughters?
Your men who fertilise you with their
steamy seed?

Attention!
Don't be stupid
Soldier
Cop
Who are you going to slay?
Your father
whose pulsing agony gave you to your
mother?

Drop that gun
Cop, Soldier
Are you going to shoot
your uncles
your tanties
your mennens
your titis
your cousins

your compays
and mackmays
your friends
who gave you a rise
when you were dead broke
the wimpering child
dreaming about milk and bread
on the parapet of hunger?

Soldier
Cop
Put the sheath on that bayonet
do not gash the guts
of the revolution
and stain the trenches
with the blood
of the patriots

Aim
Soldier
Cop
Fire!
Shoot the tyranny
fleeing from the trembling flesh
of the long-suffering people

Reverse arms
Soldier
Cop
Do not mash the revolution
with your big boots
mourn the passing of the brave
lift your helmet
and shade your eyes
from the overwhelming sun.

Farham Hannan

The Way You Are

It's the way you live, not the way you talk,
Not the way you preach, but the way you walk
that the world will judge, whatever you claim,
That the world will praise, or the world will blame.

It's the way you do, not the things you say,
Not the way you spend, but the way you pay,
It will like the least, to like the most.
It's the way you work, not the way you boast.

It's the way you sing, not the way you sigh,
Not the way you whine, but the way you try
That will hold you down, or will help you far;
Not the way you seem, but the way you are.

Rustom B Irani

Rustom B Irani was born in London and is of Persian (Zorastrian) ancestry. He studied at Cambridge University and is currently working as a Researcher with the BBC. His first book of poems, Poemgirl is due to be published next year by the Dangaroo Press (UK).

On Entering a Home for Mentally Handicapped Children

Mountains moved I was
And handicapped by a running hug
From a dribble-strewn child. Stunted
We both were, me more. Blushed
By this blatant beauty, this commotion
Of emotion, this lustful innocence, I
Caressed her tight; moat leapfrogged.
Other abandoned smiles sprinted
To my new face, pop-starred to their world.
She gripped my hand, her castle;
Sieged. I, a pied piper without a tune
Hemmed in by a throng of song; cornered
My first-caught sat skulking (?) sulky.
Looming across the hall, a solemn Gullivered
Hand.

"Seeking someone else..."

Seeking someone else, I ask you
Where you are hiding spring;
Hoping that you may change
My mind: pull flowers out of a hat;
Laugh; blossom; or some such thing.

Stunted in your safety, I beg you
Ambush me with kisses;
Spring out of winter,
Jump: leapfrogs and piggy in the middle,
Intercept my heart before it reaches what it misses.

"I have foibles and friends..."

I have foibles and friends,
And a heart that mends
When trod upon; and boots,
And words that nothing suits,
And a skin the sun has shone.

I have pains and singing,
And a mind that's springing
Always to where; and doors,
And dreams that lay down laws,
And parents bound to my care.

I have darkness and moonlight,
And a God that feels right
None of the time; and conscience,
And laughter that worships nonsense,
And youth with a valley to climb.

I have chains and freedom,
And a career that is seldom
If ever pursued; and resolutions,
And a soul that breathes two nations,
And a madness of old my birth renewed.

a(i)m

What I am (?) to write about –
(and) girls and poemgirls
and poemlove;
    and maybe love
and sex and science, and scripture,
and sad simple things
    that cryd oubt.
To know (and show) the inside
Language
    English out

Olive Irechukwu
Olive Irechukwu, 19, is studying for a Psychology degree at the City of London Polytechnic. She enjoys reading, painting and the theatre and has been writing for four years.

Life in our Beautiful Metropolis

The cold violent wind ravaged about me
settling the evil grime on my body
in my mind
on my thinking.
The rain pelted down, triumphant,
defeating me, transforming me into a sodden angry
heap. I trundled on.

The thought of clean fresh crisp air
flitted through my mind.
I refused to acknowledge this mocking reminder.

Hot, greasy, slimey – tragic bodies pressed
themselves against me. I fought the repulsion
the overriding nausea and remained conscious.

It was the rushing which struck me.
Infinite sad faces with unseeing eyes.
Imperitive to get to nowhere and even more so
to get back.

I stood in the middle of both streams
refusing to get sucked in.

Climbing the damp stony uninviting stairs,
the path to my haven, to sit in the warm security of
womb thinking of the days events
and the week still to get through.

This waging war of survival was a constant one
but with Life continually cheating
I had decided to win.
It was either survive or be crushed
and I was not yet ready to relinquish my plot
in this world.

Mehjabin-Havva Jusuf
Mehjabin-Havva Jusuf, 19, was born and educated in Walthamstow, London, where she works as a Secretary. She describes herself as a Gujarati Indian Muslim and hopes one day to be able to write poetry as fluently in Urdu as she does in English.

The Moon

The moon is like a pendulum that will not sway.
It suspends in the air giving the world the light of day. Its light like a needle pierces my eyes.
Yet, this needle's thread holds the world in its ties.

How round and golden, like the yolk of an egg,
hung in the sky like a lantern without its peg.
Its light so gentle, so wonderfully bright.
Perhaps it's been left there, perhaps it's someone's kite.

Through the window, the circle glows upon my face,
as this needle and thread sew my eye lashes together like lace.
The sky will always keep this beautiful ball through the night,
and when it disappears, I will enjoy the morning's light.

Aaron Kans

Aaron Kans, 20, was born and raised in Gravesend, Kent. A Hindu, of Punjabi origin, he is currently studying Economics at Birmingham University.

The Meaning of Life (Volume One)

"Aaron, what's the meaning of life?"
Well, let's see...
>Fred Astaires and millionaires,
>J.M. shades and silk cut flares,
>Oriental designs and recliner chairs,
>Jumping queues and skipping fares.

"Could you expand on this a bit?"
>She's like heaven on earth, poetry in lotion
>But now there's nothing between us (except an ocean)
>When "not tonight" means never again,
>And "just good friends" means it's the end.

"Go on. Go on."
>And you know when times are bad,
>When you miss the things you've never had,
>Every chord you play's a C sharp minor,
>You lose a friend and can never find her.

"Is that it? Is that all?"
>No, of course there's more to life than this...but not much more.

>So let's make this precious.

Poetry

At school
I was taught
that poetry is meant to rhyme
but in an attempt to achieve synchronicity
in words
the meaning was lost.

Having matured
I realise
that poetry is life
which may not rhyme
but has reason
and there lies its symmetry.

On the Sidelines

Hey you!
Eyes sore
from witnessing life's injustice.
Mouth languid.
Too many times,
promising to speak out,
to shout,
to scream,
to break out of fear's prison.
Instead keeping lips tight –
until the next time.
Conceiving excuses
to alleviate guilt.
Excuses known to all of us.
Finally resorting to a good book
and prayer.

Dilemma of the Black Man
(For mine, and all fathers)

Never enough time
to emerge from the mire,
life requesting too much energy.
Existing as in quicksand,
forever grasping
branches which break
and muddy banks which dissolve under fingernails.
Mind distorted by overactivity,
continually searching for truth
and attempting to make sense of the ridiculous.
Haunted into searching for an alternative meaning
in every sentence, smile and friendly gesture.
Lured by hypocrisy,
spurned by bureaucracy.
Setting fires to cleanse
and airing grievances to suspend
threads maintaining broken hearts and lives.

I'm Watching You

I'm watching you,
fingers crossed.
Watching you –
fighting on
in this "democracy".
Your efforts thwarted,
success rewarded
by patronisation and
humiliation of spirit.

I'm watching you,
fingers crossed,
while you assert
some definition of manhood.
So hurt and misunderstood.
Yours, a hard life
with little faith and less trust.

I'm watching you,
fingers crossed and see beyond
your cocky walk
and confident smile
that signals that you're far from home
and biding time.

I'm watching you,
fingers crossed,
as you fuck over another black sister,
leaving her with child and promises.

I'm watching you.
Fingers crossed
that some awful fate befall you.
It is not hate but...
I know of your anguish,

battered ego and misguided macho-istic pride
but is that excuse enough?

The Lovers

I imagined them at night,
her brown skin beneath his white.
As wisps of blond hair rest
on taut mahogany breast,
hollow eyes reminisce.
And in a flash of removed emotion
despise what's gone before.
Scenes during the day
are now replayed
and now she affords her head to rise
and chest to billow in perverted pride.
By night she has recovered
from the whispers she was meant to hear
and the grimaces employed to fan her fear.

Rejection

Pinky-white flesh,
he chose to caress.
While mauling her black skin,
he pleasured the pale one
and talked of spirit, (not colour!)
his excuse he sought a woman,
and not a mother.
Looking into grey or blue eyes,
his member and ego rose,
while brown eyes "disposed him of manhood".

He sought golden skin
and straighter hair,
his consciousness thin,
unculturally aware.
Pale through to white
were images of his dream,
black he found trite,
not befitting his scheme.

The New Woman

I lit the fire for myself,
not for you,
but I did not,
nor do I,
begrudge you comforting yourself
in its warmth,
in its purity,
in its passion.

Haida Khan
Haida Khan was born in Trinidad and educated in
England and Pakistan. She was formerly editor of
Pakistan Tourist World and Flamboyant Holiday
Journal and is considered to be one of Pakistan's
most outstanding women writers.

Delicate as a Flower (Haayat Vizier)

A Sylph-like Annissa passed me by,
As delicate as a flower;
Petal-soft skin, eyes like a gazelle
Slender-soft Saudi features had she:
My heart skipped a beat, as she walked by.

She moved as gently as a desert breeze
When Zephyr suddenly helped me to see;
Her henna-dyed hands wheat-like and olive,
Intricately woven pattern of wind and sand,
Love moves with her tribes, throughout the land.

Sybilant and chaste she moves amongst Beduins,
Camels and sheep in pastoral origins
Far, far away from cities and towns
And wilderness and solitude together abound.

With a gentle and prevailing force,
She is intent upon a course of wandering
Timelessly through thousands of years,
Of traditions, in bitter-sweet cup of immortality.

Pure gentle doe-eyed Beduwii,
Blushing unseen in this desert waste;
Heaven is reflected in your face,
Like consecrated nectar in an Elysian glade.

Payal Khurana
Payal Khurana was born in Zambia
and brought up in England. She lives in
London where she is studying for an
MA in Religious Studies. Her future
plans include relocation to India to set
up an orphanage.

Reminder of Reality

Laser-like sun rays relentlessly break
the land. The cracks widen thirsting for rain
to splash the monotony of the drought bane.
Sap-dried earth, shrivelled shrubs and dried lakes.

The effect
of the land
is mirrored on the people
with their rapidly wrinkling skin
their sunken eyes and sunken hope.

Seemingly insatiable poverty
spreads like a malignant disease, eroding
one part of mankind. As devastating
as the continent is large. "Our duty?"

Sonya King
*Sonya King, 21, was born in West
Germany to Guyanese parents. The
inspiration for her poetry is drawn
largely from her own observations of
the people around her, and is often
coloured by memories of her time
spent in Guyana.*

Poverty Song

The children
they are weeping
my love
through the rafters
the wind
is seeping
from the cold winter's night
evolves a foggy
winter's morn
snow
no greenery
trees forlorn

The blankets
they are wearing thin
my love
age has left
it's mark
the wind seeps in
the rafters
... our heaters ...
devoid of fuel
devoid of flame
devoid of life

Amidst this
we are together
my love
though our thoughts
are now dim
though our chances
now thin
we have warmth
in our love
no more hunger pangs
we feel
no more cold
suffering has peaked bold
no more pain
yet faintly, distantly
I hear
the children crying

I Remember a Young Woman

I remember a young woman
riches in personality
happy
in bloom
herding her flock
rejoicing
with her spouse
I remember a young woman
A young woman wooed

I remember a young woman
torn apart
a broken heart
a petal seemingly withered
I remember the tears
the fears
weakened and feeble
in her sorrows
broken
in her gloom
the existence of another
in her spouse's room
I remember a young woman
A young woman spurned

I remember a young woman
strengthened by life
coaching her offspring
a strong woman
successful
brilliant
admired
a hardened countenance

happy yet not happy
I remember that woman
wounded
by experience
healed
by inner strength
A woman of substance
A woman worshipped

I remember a woman
healed by time
Now a strong woman

Melissa Lambert
Melissa Lambert, from Nottingham, is
13 and the following poem won her a
first prize of £50 in the NASUWT
Anti-Apartheid Competition.

We'll Fight For Our Rights

You people,
You come into our lives and treat us as sub-humans,
For no reason you despise us, and mistreat all of our
    children.
You think to South Africa yours are a help and ours
    a hindrance,
But who cares what you think of us, who cares what
    you say.
We'll fight for our rights and condemn apartheid.

You people,
You think that we're dirty and you're full of
    hygiene,
You say that we're untidy and you are always clean,
We know you hate being near us because you think
    you'd catch something.
But who cares what you think of us, who cares what
    you say.
We'll fight for our rights and condemn apartheid.

You people,
You make our children go to second rate schools,
Because you think yours are clever and you think
    ours are fools.
Everywhere we go there are notice boards and rules.
But who cares what you think of us, who cares what

112

you say.
We'll fight for our rights and condemn apartheid.

You people,
You don't want us in your homes, because you say
we'll mark your floors.
You say that you hate us but we won't hear it
anymore.
Now you're separating our families and that's the
last straw.
The more you deny us the greater our attack.
You thought we were cowards but we'll soon be
fighting back.
All my brothers and sisters unite and we will run
amok.
In a sudden rage of anger we'll gain back all our
rights.
And you won't have time to show us rules you won't
have time to fight.
No you won't have time to show us rules you won't
have time to fight.

Archives

These are the archives of
celestial beings
take wings and
fly.
Descending like
caterpillars
in black.

Gangway

Direct eyes
singing aloud
but nothing coming
out.
Seeking newness,
the white gloved hands
the hatted head,
the last savings for
the new dress
before slipping town.

Archives

Ravaged and adrift.
Eyes yearning.
Blank.
Eyes of succinct
madness.
The great sea dragon
opens its gaping
mouth.
Treading its tongue

like water
you dislodge yourself
from its teeth.

Archives

Crumpled and worn
The eyes are vacant
The smiles worn.
Like foals they are
unfolding,
tumbling forward.
But these archives are
worn
dusty
and almost
fading.
Yet they remain,
consistently
evocative.
I'm staring at
Archives.

Begging Bowl

You come with your begging bowl
charity will not eschew
missionary brew,
a good deal of austere derision
a few dollars here
to build a water pump.
Innoculate your children
third world first.
Miserly mocks your vision.

You come with your begging bowl
one lean youngster,
deformed by hunger,
stripped by pestilence
and disease.
A woman's breast
sagging,
baby crying at
nipple. Eyesore.
Functional misery.

You come with your begging bowl
the IMF and world bank
at your door
like hungry wolves.
How ridiculous their
howling sounds.
The money lenders are
the money grabbers in
disguise.

Cry. Fall. Cry. Fall.
Irrational acquiescence

development or
underdevelopment
is no choice.
You come with your begging bowl
Demoralised.

Trilogy

SUMMER:
A bowl of orange sun
tints a clear blue sky
a staccato of children laughing
red earth beneath black feet
red hot sun glistening on shiny black backs
underneath a mud hut
Hausa, Yoruba, Mandigo children are nourished
by the gruel the earth sprouts. The red, the green,
the orange glows a gargantum of suffusion
animals stroll the emerald green forest.
The hunters are hunting
the chanters are chanting
the dancers are dancing
A boy and girl walk the ritual tightrope to
MANHOOD... WOMANHOOD

WINTER:
Leafing through the jungle, up the trees, over
the rivers, down the gorges and up to the mountains,
comes a curdling warriors' cries
a crescendo of animals react in mourning.
A young strong people alive
a refined stillness
is irreversibly broken.
The white light of oppression has fallen on black
kingdom
Africa layed outstretched
panting
vulnerable
subdued
a mother giving birth to humanity
a long virile arm touched the scorching birth
snatched a bleeding child.
The taste of flesh and blood

the smell of iron shackles.
An anchored ship awaits its sombre catch of
summer.
ENSLAVEMENT

SPRING:
Don't bother me now
let me try and pick this steadfast thorn from my
bloody flesh.
Once it corroded my flesh
the pus had flowed
it carried me over oceans of bile.
They said it was a pain I had to bear for
Humanity
Progress
Civilisation
Now I hear the past calling
but it lies in disguise
I hear my dignity calling but it is denied me.
My identity lies clandestine
I hear Africa calling
come seek me out
come seek me out
I await you motherless child.
Come seek me out.
I await your
REBIRTH

Mathanan Maharasingam

"Amidst the cruelty of war, poverty, racism and ill-health, the words of rebellion to it all must pour forth from freedom and justice. So I write, so we must all write our dreams for peace and equality – sedition is a creative act."

My India

"Go East young man," an old man said,
"Do not run, walk or fly but travel in your head."
What did he mean, that grinning sage?
My eyelids folded and my thoughts migrated.
Dusty lands and distant hums filled this space,
I danced and sang, my blood simply bubbled.
Dusky faces stared through innocent eyes,
Eyes that smiled and never hated.
The sun refused to burn at dawn or dusk
Still my body sweated an ancient musk.
To travel at heights too dizzy to breathe,
Speeding past light and misplacing one's voice,
Tickling birds' feathers, while they plucked
A hair or two of mine,
Scooping handfuls of snow from passing mountain
    tops.
My eyes so large and eager, snapping vision here
    and there,
A land of day and equal night,
A land of left and also right,
Oh such balance in this land
Where man sat childlike
In the palm of nature's hand.

Stars and Stripes

Stars and stripes and sanitised skin wipes,
The desirous spirit comes, offering and proffering,
Enfeebling the truth
Driving in chauffered wagons, speed and greed,
Pouring thoughts of glittering "oughts",
Demanding no pause, inventing no exit doors,
Casting no doubt, where doubt should yell,
Muting a church tower, where one heard a warning
bell. Men in dog collars, now collarless dogs,
Seduce their women, quite simply prey, in perfume
fogs. I see them coming, stars and stripes.
Safer smalls, noises and further uses,
Advancement in form yet decreasing in norm.
Riotous good looks, blow wild as the chinook;
The Red Indian land has truly bitten the sand,
Tasting the dust of a western lust,
No humilty in hearts,
Defiling in files and piling in piles,
Printing money all quite unfunny,
Only to spend around the bend,
Go mad on enquiry, pausing; then dig deep
For the plastic curse in your purse.
Numbers for words, so simple to compute,
Laser line logic sucked through a chute,
Dumped on waste of endless haste,
What will happen, if stars and stripes are ours to
taste? I know not that, but unlike you folk
I shan't eat for fear of that spiked drug choke.
I can't run much faster, as I may fall. And then
I may lay open to the retribution of them all.
So with wisdom my cloak, I slip through the night,
Aware through eyes beaming left then right,
Beefburger hoardings and whory boardings,
I do see but not need,

For to taste all this would mean fostering the unholy
    seed,
The seed which just left, will leave me bereft
Of my inner breath, light and water,
This hunger growth, eats all my soul,
Growing its spiky bony limbs,
And excreting fantasy whims, which chase the
    greater sins.
So people of all worlds link strength and Unite,
Hold forth your voices and from without to within
Shout and rechant "I shall not lie down, be
    blinkered in din,"
And burst the starry striped balloons with one
    heavenly pin.
And all you will see is nothing but hot air within.

To a Friend

I heard you are now mad, my friend,
But my whispers tell me,
You have arrived at wits end.
You shall be chastened, jacketed then packeted,
In a red brick church, where vallium needles lurk,
Pumping and squirting dogmatic sense,
Their patrons hedging bets and sitting on that
bloody fence,
I hope you will be freed from the incarcerating law,
I hope you shan't mummify in a vault in that
Screaming, spittle web tomb. Doctors and nurses
Thinking of weekly pay cheque purses
Will talk, scrub, grimace and feed,
But are you aware of their own inadequate need?
Do they see your soul? An innocent thing,
Writing lyrics and waiting to sing.
The sunshine of ours feeds the flowers,
Strings their petals and beckons the growth,
Raindrops bounce, hiccup and flounce,
Dive for cover, bathing our mother earth.
These I pray you see, if only for you and me.
Does anyone care? Do they have heart to spare?
If they do, then will they dare,
When all else is dark and distant.
Go within, and chant with insistence,
Go without and catch the wind, blowing
The note of an unknown thought.
With your fingers dig deep in the rich wish soil
Smell the holy formula of all creation.
You see, there is a light, the light within us all,
Which shines at the end,
Where grass and leaves sway in glebes,
Streams and beams tickle all themes,
So please pass through and take my hand,
Waiting open and warm.

But for now, the journey is for you alone
So I caress you in my love, and await
Your shimmering hungry reach.

Because They Talk

When you hear them quarrelling,
And knocking themselves over,
Yes, when they're travelling
Or bent over the Passover,
Know it's all
Because they talk.

When dogs bent over a bone
Snarl, bite and bark
Or writhe and grumble while alone
Or race about in the dark,
Know it's all
Because they talk.

When secrets are given away,
And domestic strife takes hold
And even the cat can't play,
While hatred sparkles like gold,
Know it's all
Because they talk.

But when the silent worm on his watery way
Is attacked, captured and killed
By black brutal ants as catch for the day,
Even when the worm with tranquillity was filled,
Shall we pretend it's all...
Because they talk?

Preethi Manuel
Preethi Manuel is a Lecturer in Media
Studies at Goldsmiths' College,
London. She arrived in Britain from
India as a teenager in 1974 and her
deep association with her birthplace
provides much of the inspiration for
her writing. A visual interpretation of
the following poem was made recently
into a 4 minute video.

Ma, Ma, Khana

Ma
Ma
Khana
You cry in your sleep my child

You toss
and turn
and lick your lips as if on my breast
but I have no food
Swami Nanda he has hidden some
but to buy I have no means
In vain I dig for roots
in the parched
cracked earth
but there is none
there is none
none
the Gods
they have failed again
Ten thousand grains of sand
slip through my fingers
my child
my child
you are

hungry
but I have
no food
ma
ma
khana

Christibell Nicholas
Christibell Nicholas, 24, grew up in
Grenada, but currently lives in East
London.

Watching and Waiting

When you wait for death
You've given up hopes and wishes,
Accepted the inevitability of life,
Acknowledged the extinguishing light.
Watching, waiting for a man to die.

Sitting, waiting,
I remember the chair was hard
The ward stark but busy.
Nurses scurrying back and forth.
Watching, waiting for a man to die.

Memories flooded through:
His enjoyment of life, sense of humour,
The journey we all began together.
Now his journey's end.
Watching, waiting for a man to die.

I concentrate on his pulsating neck,
The shallow breathing.
Then spewing from his mouth life itself.
Slowly it sank into my brain.
I need wait no more.

Another dies.
Caught in the tragedy of justice.
But he will always live
Alive and fresh in our memories.
Meanwhile the struggle goes on.

128

Joseph Nicholas
Joseph Nicholas was born in Roseau,
Dominica, in 1926, and came to Britain
in 1952. A fellow of Cambridge
University and former Fleet Street
journalist, he enjoys bright company,
travel, reading and classical music.

The Charge of the Light Brigade

I

Half a league, half a league,
Half a league onward,
All in the valley of Death
Rode the six hundred.
'Forward, the Light Brigade!
Charge for the guns!' he said;
Into the valley of Death
Rode the six hundred.

II

'Forward, the Light Brigade!'
Was there a man dismayed?
Not tho' the soldier knew
Some one had blundered:
Their's not to make reply,
Their's not to reason why,
Their's but to do and die:
Into the valley of Death
Rode the six hundred.

III

Cannon to right of them,
Cannon to left of them,
Cannon in front of them
Volleyed and thundered;
Stormed at with shot and shell,

Boldly they rode and well,
Into the jaws of Death,
Into the mouth of Hell
Rode the six hundred.

IV

Flashed all their sabres bare,
Flashed as they turned in air,
Sabring the gunners there,
Charging an army, while
All the world wondered:
Plunged in the battery-smoke
Right thro' the line they broke;
Cossack and Russian
Reeled from the sabre-stroke
Shattered and sundered.
Then they rode back, but not,
Not the six hundred.

V

Cannon to right of them,
Cannon to left of them,
Cannon behind them
Volleyed and thundered;
Stormed at with shot and shell,
While horse and hero fell,
They that had fought so well
Came thro' the jaws of Death
Back from the mouth of Hell,
All that was left of them,
Left of six hundred.

VI

When can their glory fade?
O the wild charge they made!
All the world wondered.
Honour the charge they made!

Honour the Light Brigade,
Noble six hundred!

Alfred, Lord Tennyson

The Brixton Riot

I

Half a league, half a league,
Half a league onward,
All in the Valley of Death
Fought the Black Hundred.
Forward the Black Brigade!
Charge for the cops he said:
Into the Valley of Death
Fought the Black Hundred.

II

Forward the Black Brigade!
Was there a black dismayed?
Remember those slavery days
Not that their children knew
Some one had blundered:
Ours not to make reply
Ours not to reason why
Ours but to do and die
Into the Valley of Death
Fought the Black Hundred.

III

Copper to right of them,
Copper to left of them,
Copper in front of them
Tear-gas and shielded;
Stormed at like mad like hell
Boldly they fought and well
Into the jaws of Death
Into the Mouth of Hell
Fought the Black Hundred.

IV

Flashed all their cutlass bare
Flashed as they jumped in air
Shield and bobby charging bare,
Charging an enemy
While all the world wondered.
Plunged into tear-gas smoke
Right through the line they broke.
Chief constables, bled from
Cutlass-stroke shattered and
Sundered they ran and back, but not,
Not, the Black Hundred.

V

Copper to right of them,
Copper to left of them,
Copper behind them,
Volleyed and thundered while
Blacks, our heroes fell, while
house and business melt.
They that had fought so well
Came through the Jaws of Death.
Back from the Mouth of Hell,
All that was left of them
Left of the Black Hundred.

VI

When can their glory fade?
Think of the charge they made!
All the world wondered.
Honour the charge they made!
Honour the Black Brigade.
Noble Black Hundred!

Allison E Patoir,
Allison E Patoir, 21, is from Sand
Hills, Guyana. Her hobbies include
singing, reading and corresponding
with her pen-friends.

If with Pleasure

If with pleasure you are viewing
The work a man is doing
If you like him or you love him
Tell him now.

Don't withold your approbation
Till the preacher makes oration
And he lies with snowy lilies on his brow.
For no matter how you shout it
He won't really care about it,
He won't know how many teardrops
You have shed.

If you think some praise is due him
Now's the time to slip it to him
For he cannot read his tombstone
When he's dead.

Prayer-Song

Jah, thanks for the life that I have.
Thanks for the breath that you give me each day,
Thanks for the gift of sight to see
The beauty of your scenery.

Jah, thanks for the life that I have.
Thanks for the faith that sees me through,
Thanks for the patience to go through each day
In a conscious, living and loving way.

Jah, thanks for the life that I have.
Thanks for the great way you've shown me your
love,
Thanks for the blessings you've given to me,
In this time, faith in you will set me free.

Jah, thanks for the life that I have.
Thanks for the glimpse of a better tomorrow,
Thanks for the comfort and warmth that comes
From you Jah, to your daughters and sons.

Tasneem Qadir
Tasneem Qadir, 17, is a young writer
who draws his inspiration from his
knowledge of Soviet history. He
structures his poems thematically
around the season of winter.

Twist of Tauras

Slow wind blow through years to the snow
How can a lie be a depth away
When we reach within to withdraw our winter
So wind blow against the funnels of the mind,
So wind hit harshly against our palm lines,
How can the truth be in shoddy despair?
Opened the window the snow settled there.

Cold desert storm cut through the rain
Soaked us in again and again,
How can the winds refuse to pipe their chant?
Especially now after what they have brought,
A frozen, darkened breeze smothered us in the
night; we wrestled with the moon
To bring back some light.

Slow reaching storms, ice fingers across the sky.
Out there in woodland jungle we hear a howling cry,
A month which stretches for many years,
A month which sheds only tears.
Into the pools of life the water and wine
Which drown in winter and darkened lullabys,
Into the month which will never end
Where storm clouds unwind and start to send.

When I walked upon that path of orange littered
leaves,
I walked past the brown disfigured towering trees
Relaxing in the warmth of pale cameo walls

136

Fires twisting turning, bringing out its warmth,
Pitying human nature, something we have to bear,
Outside there's someone alive but not living.

Speckles of frost scattered all around.
Tavern lights were lit as we staggered out of town.
How can we sweat and toil after this taste?
Which freshened our lives; it must be our fate.
How can we work after tasting this wine?
Which showed up the history of all mankind.

Dreams of Interception

What is important is that moment in time
Revealed in a horizon beyond the outline,
What was important was the real illusion,
We stretched our thinking to points of confusion.

Me, Mercas, Feste, all my friends
Watching a skyline of a red orange blend,
We see the beauty in the glow of the sky
Glowing around skyscrapers and shapes on high –
From filters shaded in a hazy form,
We look at the angles and shapes from our room:
Me and all my friends in a room full of time
Watching the sunset drifting behind.

We notice its beauty, we notice its view,
The spectrum of colours held in front of you.
We point at the shimmers and nebulous forms
Shrouding the buildings in heat of the sun:
We see America from a window afar,
Crystalised America – a shining star.

We notice its beauty, we notice its view,
Here in a momentary illusion of time.
Why do the words crumble as I sketch the next line?
Why do I feel confused as to where I should be?
Divorcing this moment of my history.
Why do I need to see this is done?
Why do I have to look at the sun?

The sun with its forms red orange and pale,
A crust of a dream I saw in the shade.
Why do figures weave spells of illusion?
Why have my friends hijacked this confusion?
That moment in time when we saw the sun melt

And red orange colours rippled onto the set,
We looked with our eyes and toasted this life,
Oh comrades of honour drink up your wine!

The Coloured Face

The coloured face like a mark of disgrace
Peering from crowds of millions,
All uniform in white but I am disliked
Because of the mask of continents.

The coloured face like dirt against snow
Is a mask of thought which never shows,
Take off the mask and reveal the light –
Show your face to the shining daylight.

Tasneem you have lived for just being you,
Let no-one change the way you are true.
So cast off cosmetics and surgical device –
This is the face of pure daylight.

The coloured face is like a room in the dark,
Is dyed by colours which flow hard and fast,
Let no-one discolour the natural tone –
Lighten the shade and reach the bone.

In a crowd you may feel a little strange,
Staring at faces which all look the same,
But never fear because your strength is here –
To rise up against any hatred.

Nazalee Raja

Human Failure

Where does innocence go when lost?
Are we maimed, like a flower by frost?
And all the dreams of yesteryear
Are hardened when they fail to appear.
When we want too much
And want it too soon
What price do we pay for each tear?

When seeking out hearts desire
To such great heights we aspire
But when hopes don't materialise,
When the truths all become lies,
And everything relied on
Turns upside down
How much do we learn to despise?

I'm Tired

I'm tired, Lord,
So tired.
It's hard to feel inspired
When you're drained of all emotion
And you simply have no notion
As to what life's all about.
In the end all I know is
I'm so tired!

Don Ricketts
Jamaican born Don Ricketts is a
freelance Writer and Graphic Artist and
has lived most of his life in Jamaica
until his recent relocation to Miami,
USA. Writing since 1970, he has had
his works published in such journals as
Caribbean Quarterly *and* Caribbean
Review. *He is currently preparing his*
six part book of poetry entitled 20th
Century Vision.

A Woman I Knew

City-Kingston
I see you
now in your face;
cosmetic-painted onto reality,
layers of facaded progress
implied in glimpses on flash
and solid,
earthy groundations.

The tram-line stitches have been
removed from your face-
the streets bleed like life,
and the pneumo-drill's spasms are
still needling your past,
your ass patching your pride.

Again you grin at that
that-ole-whore port royal
with your gold-filled skyscraper smile,
in your waterfront style;
her hustling days are over, drowned
in her unchaste waters,

143

you wait only on your next lover.
(Will he be a redman, instead of white,
of a more timely import, but nevertheless
for lesser-developed-cuntries only...
or, will he be black, blacker still...
like a Garvey?)

I wait too, me sperm-man
watching to see you explode with this fruit
of my ancestors, transplanted and left, growing
inside your mysteries,
watered in time,
growing.
And I will not be rejected lightly, lover!

Keith

Keithie,
you did not always want to play
hide-and-seek, police-and-tief
it seems you were seeing something we did not see
yet, (I know now).
And in our games, I remember
I sometimes tensed a senseness in you
– of you watching from behind your eyes inside your
brain,
reminding you
not to get rough with us, especially me.

I am remembering the things I remember, then
as now you must have felt the hole in our waiting
on time to pass between the years,
tense as the walls between the lanes of concrete
wherein our boyhood adventures wandered,
touching our minds in our brains the picture
of this great future.

I know now.
That you were going to meet the man. The man
Babylon.
That layer we intuited above our lives, that lid
that shut down on our prayers.
All those prayers
we felt inside more than those we said
in all the high vaulted Sunday afternoons
of John Wesley's deliverance formula.

I didn't understand the holiness of mystery then
I don't understand the mystery of holiness now.

I know now that that conjurer's trick helped
to fuck up our lives, and our brothers and sisters'
chances with life.
Those haven't changed much with the jump of time
to now.

When I saw your face again today
sitting old, looking tired
like your father in the times before the wasting away
of his brutal beautiful strength
on the piers, on the docks of Kingston
Jesus, how we are crucified
Christ, the tears are hot
inside my face.

I cannot cry
You wouldn't understand my averted stare.
You were brother to me, brother-man,
when I knew not any blood kinship.
I can only make my memory my hair-shirt,
my dedication.

Carnavaal '84

Kitch singing,
Perez Prado-like
'Mambo Alma...'
Soca fevah jamming tight,
No disco please, tonite
In the union of students, workers and youth
Amid the brief flash of Caribbean man-light flaring.
Bachannal threading a slender connection
Thru' the crowd
Hands high exulting, jamming
Soca rhythm stepping, stringing
A jumping live-wire connection from Venezuela
To New Orleans
Via a road march of islands.
We shakin' we ass
All over de place
We shakin' we ass
All up in they face
Of dem who ent hearin' Black Stalin
Or Kitch
Or even Prado.

We celebrating the vigor of we men
We celebrating the compassion of we women
We celebrating the hope of we unity
For all we children.

So while we struggles continue
We also march, to the sound of steel drums
Don't stop the tempo.
Jam one for Grenada!

Easter

I

This crown of thorns
Encircling conscience
Prickly as decision
Force against the tender
Flesh feelings
That enwrap.
But...
Inside the firmness
Is Love; the god
Keeping out that stage,
That pain.

This other one meets the resolve
Of reality borne upon
Shoulders stretched to ever –
Open and everliving welcome-bosom
And back
Stooped to carry
Burdens of the earth
And rocks and trees
And hands nailed
To making ends meet
At the centre of this mantime
In a space, healed together
To make
A point
in time
A banner, a standard
Raised
To mankind's choice
Where man and god meet
Eternally
In this crowd of glory.

INRI
I'n'IRI

II

The same wood, adorned
They worship
At fat santa class feast.
Log of pagan nordic hearth
Which wood he made
And fashioned
Strong and graceful
To complement rockstone's challenge
In yard and palace
Synagogue and temple.
With hands that knew
Of blood and tears
To mix
In straining sweat
To drive
And coax
And smooth
And finish to beauty.

The same wood, shorned
He works
An essence of worship
To creator. Man. God.
What creativity he blesses
And justifies
From then to now,
Caring for this garden's starving face
In north and south
And east and west
With life that suffers
From birth to tomb
But seeks
And facing dispossession
Bends yes, breaks not
And struggles, again to rise.

Materialist Doubts

With patented smile, I
impatient exile, watching captivity
the soft underbelly of Uncle c.i.a.
where she pushes her sperm out, lady libertine
into the space, racing: the dilemma
reflexive collapse
of the red-what-and-blue plastic bubble
happy bicentenary seventy-six,
you know, revolution and all that!

The symbol of her orgasms drips waste
she pisses assault streams at the machine-gun of the
Cuban backbone,
conscious of the vulnerability of Kennedy's cape,
of her softer underbelly.

For us here in spider-land, she smiles glisteningly.
She is ripe: with the fascination of a sore
festering full and itching to burst
and cover us all with her falling-out.
Shall we go polluted into the millenium?

Guardedly, the future-place stares at us through its
two way mirror
while here, we opine strangely
and see only a vague road stretching away
back into the deep forest behind our brows.
And our cocoon has not been silky
smooth and profitably refined:
the cobwebs that tie our lashes open
are squeezed from black widows
and fighting black cocks and
angry death inside a slaver's rib cage.

This new Egypt, this Babylonia
with its pyramids and obelisks that stand on feet of
atomic fires
hopping in the heat,
leaping at space
to escape from this reality.
This image
shall not survive our exodus.

Africall

I have never seen you
neither known the massing of anciency
that suckles the superorganic growth
that you are...

I have not seen you,
yet...
personally,
thinking of you
I can only project
second-hand
hand me down
histories
(I have reclaimed them
to cover my slave-child nakedness).
A terrifyingly large thought
that throbs silently
a cosmic heartbeat
to which I, black corpuscle, run.

Meaningless without your being
I have never seen you
but I feel you
insistent behind my brain
glowing inside by skin, darkly.

"I don't believe this"

I don't believe this;
I've done it again.
But how? I was so careful.
I only used it when I needed to
And sometimes I even went without,
Surely there's some mistake?
But no, I've read it over and over again,
They're right, I know deep down that they are.

What shall I do now?
I'll have to go home, break the news,
Tell him before they do,
They'll be writing it now.
I'll tell him after dinner, he'll be in a good mood
then,
Perhaps he'll help me out,
He has to, after all if I can't handle it
The responsibility falls on him.
It will be alright, we'll manage
Of course we will,
I mean it's not the first time I've been overdrawn.

Sajjad H Shamsi
Sajjad H Shamsi spent many years in
the Kenyan civil service before retiring
as Head of the Asian Service, Kenya
Broadcasting Corporation, and coming
to Britain. He lost his sight in a road
traffic accident and subsequently
devotes much of his time to writing.
His first collection of Urdu poetry has
recently been published and a further
collection, of English verse, is shortly
to go to press.

The Dawn

The black of night has silently lifted
To reveal the fair face of a new dawn
The Emperor of Light driving a golden chariot
Sallies forth to review his domains
The frontiers of darkness fold away
The tiny lamps of the night
Pay their homage to the Great Orb
And silently retire
Song birds sound a fanfare to welcome the King
Blossoms offer their bejewelled lips
To be kissed by shafts of golden light
The morning breeze showers petals in his path
And leaves a mist of fragrance in its wake
The heart of the universe throbs with life
Man and beast and insects
Wasps and bees and glittering butterflies
All hasten to their appointed stations
This then is the Dawn – the beginning of all things
The Dawn of the Day, the Dawn of History, the
Dawn of Life

I Am No Judge

In my life of over three score and ten
I have met all manner of men
Some were godly, saintly and pure
Very reserved, very shy and demure
Correct in action, speech and mind
Well disposed, humble and kind,
Others debonair, well dressed and wise
I found rather hard to see through their disguise
They were so vain, treating others like dirt
Every act an injury, every word a hurt
With no morals, no ethics, no creed
As if they belonged to another breed
Everyone I met, I judged and analysed
Some I liked and some I despised
Yet I never pondered my own case
The thought came to me as a boot to the face!
What if others judge me as I judged them
For I am no pearl, no nugget, no gem!

Jenneba Sie Jalloh

The Promised Land

Dedicated to Dennis Brown's *The Promised Land*
and to all exiles in a foreign land, who dream of, or
remember a safer, better place.

A stranger to Africa.

I know that upon reaching your shores
Africa, my spiritual home...
I will find a culture different from the one I'm used
to
A music different from the one I'm used to hearing
A people who see me as apart, not a true African
born.

But as an African, born in a foreign land,
I must have something to dream of – something to
believe in
I must feel there is a safer place,
Even if I never reach there myself...

AFRICA

A stranger, an "English person"
But while I'm here, Africa, land of contradictions,
Suffering, starvation... first and greatest
civilisation...

Hope... my father's land
Give me something to dream upon.

I may eventually find... disillusionment,
But for now, in England, so cold, so unwelcoming
Let Africa be...

THE PROMISED LAND

Durlabh Singh
Durlabh Singh, from London, is a
Graphic Artist and Poet. He has given
poetry readings throughout the
London area and has contributed
poems, cartoons, articles and
photographs to a variety of journals
and newspapers.

The Moon

The moon
Oh catch the moon
Put a noose in its nose
Bring it back to harness
The icy wilderness of the moon
Sprinkle it with flowered dew.

Catch it before it runs
To penumbra of sun, hides itself
Oh run and run to recover
From suffocation of grief and bart
Stiffen its dust with tears
Or the ceremonial flood
Of the tidings, of the present
The anti-poetic
Peregrin of the sedged cart
The olibanum of crushed heart.

The moon
Oh catch the moon
Till it runs
To the hilliard mansions
The septic pun
Where the master of hounds sleeps
With his metallic face
Turned to the wall

157

Where under the greenish shadows
Shines the dool.
The moon
Oh catch the moon
Catch it before it runs, to the penumbra of sun.

Kiss

When I kissed you
In an arid waste of that cheek
The tangle of your hair did dissect
Indulged in making a tale brief
Of some sombre tired demise
Of hope forlorn or of rainy nights
And communications between two hearts
Flowered perhaps in meadows of grass.
Sweet whispers stopped not
A song of soul on warm lips
Neither charm away nor stop now
The wonder of love in mind's crypts.

Sonnet

Would not I carry my rugged pride
When element to element will mingle and reside.
In perfumed consummation of interstellar space
In a new planet cast out of Brahama's rage.
For ever wishing my nibbled pen could trace
A line of haughty verse to silence this deadly state
The world's affair and all its cloud-clapped might,
But ends in poor surrender shorn of Man's pride
Shorn of all honour when our tattered rags do show
The imprints of tempters all their dishonest row
Then we hate to touch our mortgaged flesh and bone
When souls are slaughtered in churchyards of rhone.
It might have been better to explore other avenues
The spirit of dark waters or other sealed venues.

Sanjay Singh

Little Innocent Eyes

Staring at me
With those eyes of yours
Waiting for a grain of hope
Waiting for an empty bowl.
Little Innocent Eyes
What did you ever do
To deserve a life like this?
A struggle like this
For survival.

Eyes that tear through my heart
Burn through my clothes
With their innocence
With their tenderness
Playing on my conscience.

Bloated stomachs fed on tears
Little Innocent Eyes
With that look of fear
What did you ever do
To deserve a hell like this?
A struggle like this
For survival.

Lemn Sissay
Lemn Sissay is shortly to publish his
first volume of poems, Tender Fingers
in a Clenched Fist, *with Bogle*
L'Ouverture. He organised the first
black writers' competition in the north-
west and is a co-founder of
Cultureword.

Tense Tattered Tortured Tried Tested and Torn

I am a tree with no roots... or dead roots... or
   chemical ridden roots
I am emotion with no colour. I am a colourless
   dream. I am a scream.
I am a tear spiked with acid that runs burning down
   tender cheeks
I am the decisive decade the moaning month, the
   harrowing hour the stretched second the
   weakest week
I am the charred twisted and broken branch of my
   grand ancestral tree
I am the burden of the recognition of something that
   never happened to me
I am the tragic trauma... tense tattered tortured
   tried tested and torn
I am still underdeveloped, without life, I am still
   born.
I am the stolen manuscript. The paper in the fire.
The unwritten anthology.
I am an ape, victimised by the poking of the iron rod
   of anthropology.
I am the maroon nightmare. The muffled cries of a
   child turning in his pillow
I am yesterday and always tomorrow... always

tomorrow... tomorrow
I am the epitome of the Western world's real dream
I am the colourless dream. I am the scream.
I am the glued together statue of a man
I am the fickle face of one in a million
I am the colourless dream. I am the Western world's
dream.
I am a scream. I am a scream. I am a scream.
I cry but then I laugh and slowly smile
I can only be a broken man........for a short while

She Read as She Cradled

You part of me

Every day your history
Every tomorrow your destiny
Every growth your mystery
Every mother wants a baby

                                             like you

Every laugh your personality
Every look your clarity
Every word your stability
Every mother wants a baby

                                             like you

Every hiccup a comedy
Every fall a catastrophe
Every worry my worry
Every step you're beside me
Every sight you're pure beauty
Every mother wants a baby

                                             like you

Every tear wiped carefully
Every word spoke lovingly
Every meal fed silently
Every cloth washed caringly
Every song sung sweetly

Every day I whisper quietly
Every mother wants a baby

                                             like you

Bad Trip – LSD

The daisy that spits pure acid
That burns pure consciousness
Darkness becomes valid
So too does unhappiness

Night creeps in with long spindle fingers
And scratches slowly in the mind
White screams haunt from soul singers
The rope begins to bind

Slow tightening sounds
White pointed masks slits for eyes
Splurting from the bubbling ground
Fire spits from the skies
Fire spits from the skies

Melts your scarred and burning face
You did the wrong thing
Wrong time wrong place
Flower with a sting
Flower with a sting

Attracted by distortion
Difference and change
Too late for disillusion
It has bound you in chains

To drown you in the river
Drown you in the sea
Turned you on to make you shiver
LSD

Turned you on to make you shiver
LSD

Negotiations

For the radical faction to change the constitution
They should take their allegations to the institution
So we took our allegations with a big bag of patience
Before we even met we felt the pain of
prejudgement
So we set up a meeting and gave the standard
greeting
And if vibes could harm us we'd have got a good
beating
But the minutes were restricted and the picture they
depicted
Was nothing but a smutter of the things we had
presented

But onward we went with constructive intention
Keeping our strengths from personal friction
But keeping the prevention of personal pretension
Was keeping construction in total detention
Resulting in destruction and bad vibrations

And a cut in the bag that was holding the patience
And a cut in the bag that was holding the patience
And a cut in the bag that was holding the patience

Nursery Rhyme

Humpty Dumpty was pushed
But propaganda played its part
And Little Jack Horner was paranoid
One word would lose his heart
So he pulled out a plum instead
To save him from winding up dead
He knew all the kings horses and all the kings men
Would never put Humpty together again

Sika Valery Small
Sika Valery Small is a Jamaican who
has been living in London since 1968.
She is a final year student at the
London School of Economics.

The Defence Rests, Your Honour

I

"Is the man in this room, madam?"
Tossing back her long brown mane
displaying the full force of her beautifully chiselled
face. Full red lips, slightly apart. Perfect white teeth.
Head high, eyes unwavering, slowly swivelling
about the room.
Resting; on the man in the dock.
Raising one long, elegant hand, she pointed a slim
finger. Paused: (The room held its breath).
When her eyes locked with his she said, with as
much venom as she could muster –
"That's him, that's the bastard who raped me."
(The room breathed out)

II

The young black man looked deep in her blue green
eyes. Impassive.
He tried not to think of the pain in his side.
Three broken ribs. Resisting arrest.
Aching head, a taste of blood. His own.
He was hungry, dirty and tired.

III

"How do you plead?" asked the clerk not bothering
to look up.
After all, he was guilty, has to be, stands to reason.
"Not Guilty."
What! "Do you fully understand what you are
saying?" his Lordship asked.
"I said, your Honour, not guilty." (The room
buzzed)

IV

One after another the witnesses came.
As each left the noose tightened.
And what did he ask them all?
"Are you positive, quite sure about the date and
time?"
Yes, of course. They seem surprised.
"The defence rests, your Honour."
(The room tittered)

V

The blue uniform was a credit.
Broad shoulders, head well back, feet apart, secure.
Oh! What a sight!
His statement was clear, precise and damning.
(The room applauded)

VI

The prosecution summed up carelessly. A formality
only. The defence began.
In a quiet unassuming voice he told the tale.
The broken door. The sound of truncheon against
something solid like bone-his own.
Reinforced boots against his head.

He told them how he thought of death, wished to
die, but they would not let him.
He told them how it took fifteen minutes to beat him
and drag him from his bed.
(The room shifted, uneasy)
His voice went on. And to sum up, he said –
At the time and place alleged I was somewhere else
instead. Prison.
(Uproar in the room. What! How?)

VII

"Why did you not say so before?"
"I was unconscious for a long time, your Honour,
since the morning of my arrest."
"But most of all," he said, "no one has ever asked
me where I was on the date and time alleged."
(The room exploded)
The man sat down
and smiled.

Hugh Stultz
Hugh Stultz was born and grew up in
Jamaica where he attended the
Jamaican School of Drama. As a poet
he strives "for a voice which echoes his
personal, cultural and artistic
heritage".

Journal of a Street Fighter

Day 1   Today I entered the streets of change
marching;
with a burning hole in my stomach
and fear gripped tightly in my hand.

Day 2   We fought the king's men all day long
they shot us down in the streets
like flies
and buried us
like dogs
I could hear the King's voice
seeping through the soil
       "there must be no compassion
           for the scum."

Day 3   My brothers wallowed
through the rising stream of blood
stumbling against the stench.
They were in search of fresh blood
to fill that hole in their stomachs.

Day 4   My spirits rose to join my brother's
victory dance
they stormed the palace,
sacrificed the King
at the altar of their suffering.
And filled the hole
in their stomachs.

Day 5   "We hope to do better,
great things,"
the brother in charge said,
against a backdrop of hungry cheers.
Heard grandpa whisper
behind the autumn leaves:
"These young leaders
must all have parrots in their throats."

Sand Story

Peel the sand
from your eyes
son
here let me
place some clay
and spit
on that wound
go
wash in the pool
look for yourself
she has gone.

Blessed are those
who have waited
without seeing.

Easter Song

Noon day blues
follow children down town
dancing in the sun
with fish bowl eyes
and pregnant smiles
arms stretched wide
for a few pieces of silver
rejection is a hole
deep in their pocket
these children bleed black
right there
on the street

Evening prayer
eli eli lama sabach thali
bow your head
in the sun children
roll inside your empty gut
sleep sweet like death
carried away
on that nightmare's
broad back
soon light
will slip
inside a corner
of the eye
force open the lid

Morning crows
coughing dust
arise
from the earth children
weak like foetus
bush tea at the altar this morning

to build strength
for the Sunday of your life
and when they come
for the rent

you are gone

Mask

After they
invaded our land
stole our masks
and broke our gods
I had no face to speak
to seek god in I self
was fear
of that dark hull
(some of us were able to smuggle our gods
inside the belly of our dreams)

in new land
long frocked christ people
blessed the place
where shackles burnt
teaching tolerance
making criss cross sign
on their naked breast
these dumb oracles had no masks

ear learnt this dumb tongue
until back
could break no more
then independence
incubated in those dark hulls
hatched in the belly of our minds
we tried to raise our gods
dance shango but

our masks were
were locked in a tomb
in their museum

now poem must become mask
pull us from the belly

of our dreams
unshackle tongue
to sing eye song and
dance freedom in the streets
for I self
and the children

the will is everything
they cannot
break our gods again

Dorothy Syme
Dorothy Syme lives in Liverpool where
she is studying part-time in preparation
for an Access course. She lives with her
ten children and has only recently
started to write poetry.

The Shops of Yesteryear

Christmas in the bakers was a busy day
as the people queued to bake their cakes
2d a time the baker said
and I'll lend you the tin
to cook it in.

Hot steaming bread was my favourite
thing, big and small as the people came.
Sunday joints as well he did
all for coppers well spent.

Slabs of butter on the grocer's counter
being beaten into shape
sugar in blue bags was oh! so grand
2 ozs of tea and one egg please.

The butcher with his pig's head
strings of sausages hanging up –
marrow bones for soup he sold
bacon pieces were good to buy.

The Cleaning Woman

It was cold, so cold,
as she poured salt on the thick ice
using a knife to rid the step
of the intruder
that stopped her scrubbing
the red brick steps.

It was still dark as she struggled
to open the heavy door
to allow the light
to stream out to the
flight of steps
which were once again
beginning to freeze over.

Next came the long wide corridors
that needed scrubbing on hands and knees.

People with disdaining looks
walked all over the floor
and paid her no heed.

Time still was not finished,
as classrooms she entered,
cleaning and polishing on hand
and knee,
till the floor looked like mirrors.

Chris Tajah
Chris Tajah, from London, is an actor.
His numerous stage roles have
included Galactic Jack in Tooth of
Crime and Simon in Redemption Song
with the Black Theatre Company.
With the Orange Tree Theatre
Company, he has played McDuff in
Macbeth and Bottom in A Midsummer
Night's Dream. Television credits
include appearances in Prospects and
Dempsey and Makepeace. Chris Tajah
is currently writing his first novel.

Feather

She colours my senses
Peaking my awareness,
My faculties are examined by her eyes,
My tone remains sharp,
All that surrounds my heightened cells
Is she.

She fills my quench cup
The severe thirst which clapped my throat
And made me hoarse
Was eased by her lips resting upon mine.
So soft the luxury of her I want to keep
Forever.

Her lips of gladness
She gave to me, and crushed
My cheerless mask.

She has before,
She will again,
Touch my hand as no other has,
As no other can.

She has a smile
It certifies to say,
Window shops night
Displays day.

She has a soul stroll motion
That swim my feelings to her,
Tide wide.

A style of pride, watch as she passes,
An erotic movement,
The truth of woman is about her flesh
A rawness of beauty.

Observe this black feather,
And rhythms conjure in the mind,
Underneath the airy summit of home
The elements and the feather
Play together.

Nothing for Nothing

There ain't no easy money.

When the rain pours
And the sun don't shine
You're looking for riches
But you'll soon realise.

There's no easy money,
If you've got your hands above your head
If you're praying out aloud
If you're crawling out of bed
If you're hollering, screaming
If you're walking on the ceiling

You want easy money.

When you go to a job interview
And they say 'Thanks for coming, but no!'
When you've got nowhere else to go,
When you can't buy food or even drink
When you need some time
Some room to think
You'll search for an easier route.

But when somebody fills your head
With schemes,
Starts pumping up your mind with dreams,
Remember, there's no easy money.

There's no quick way to living well
No quick way to fancy cars.
There's no quick way to expensive clothes,
But you can pretend to be wealthy by smoking
Plenty of big cigars,
Cough to death in style.

There ain't no easy money, no.

Take Me

Sinking in the misty blue distant ocean
Away, away.
That swaying instance.
Casually unperturbed I approach
Oh! Opaque force so wonderful
To behold.
Like an infant greets all wide-eyed
With aroused emotions simmering
I recall that first wet kiss,
Puck in preparation...

In the moonlight that shone
Through her eyes
I bathed freely,
In the touch she gave
I swayed, I tumbled into her arms
To the abandoned drifting wreckage
That was my heart.
She breathed life anew,
She untangled the strings
That held me taut
She rekindled the fire
That has never seen height so tall
Nor heat so rich.
Oh buoyant flame dance me merry.
There undraped you stood
Your hand outstretched,
Around me the walls were cold,
No longer caring I swam
Into the blue,
The blue... the blue... the blue
Into the blue.

One Day

Be married or stay single?
In the middle piggy run, run.
In the morning be there.
                    I need to seek the silent air.
Air that pumps the blood
                    Air that is exhuberant
A vigorous starting point,
                    Ours alone.
In close we are warm, snuggle up
                    Around me, hold secure.
Snooze on... on.
                    Kiss the hours away, let them go.

We'll like each other a little better
                    In the morning, we'll be tighter,
We won't be walking through maybe doors,
                    We'll be standing strong,
A confidence from shoe leather to spirit
                    Will prevent our shadows being
                    alone.

Come let's greet the air that chills
Trembling hands
Where lays our destiny.
When I place my ring
On your soft accurate hands
Express all you've saved.

Once again we hold a chance.

Sinharaja Tammita-Delgoda
Sinharaja Tammita-Delgoda is 24, and is a research student in Oriental Studies at London University. As a member of Jenako Arts Black Poets, he performs regularly and writes, he hopes, on black issues with black people in mind.

Sugar Ray Leonard: All American Boy

An Ode to Sugar Ray.
Every hero deserves his day.

Coffee-cream. American dream,
Golden Negro, he's sugar clean.

Nicotine without the Tar,
For which she looked so far.

That's Sugar Ray, he's sugar sweet.
An all-American sugar treat.

Ali, with his handsome face,
Angry platform for his race.

But Sugar Ray, his perfect face,
The perfect credit to his race.

Marvin Hagler not today,
All America will have her way.

For Reagan's golden days,
Need their sugar rays.

"Soweto"

Blood drips and drops,
It curdles, it clots.

It gathers into murky pools,
Over which the Boer drools.

Mirrored in the sticky light,
His face is gleaming white.

Red and dripping
In folds of fat,
Smiling like a cat.

A day's work done
Such good fun,
How the Kaffirs run.

Can you hear
The children scream?
Does it tear
Your waking dream?

Pools are lapping
at your door,
Tearing at
your Liberal core.

The time is past for
Liberal cries,
No more listening
To their lies.

The time has come,
To cull the Boer,
To even up,
The children's score.

He's fat and luscious,
See him swell,
Turn that spit.
Roast him well.

Oh Britannia

With me enter into the eye of a
becalmed storm.
Before us the form of britannia
withered in strength and bent in posture.
Bequeathed to it illusions of grandure
and visions of self-inflated worth.

Yet in the flicker of contact with the
eye, reflected mirror like its
perception, a britannia virile in
strength and upright in purpose.

But truth is a stranger to him who
nightmarishly hammers at his door
with messages whose effect is to
evaporate the historical mist of myth
in the name of reality
and its counterpart truth.

Abigail Weekes
Abigail Weekes, 22, was born in the
East End of London. She lived in
Trinidad for six years while a teenager
and has been writing poetry since the
age of eleven. She is a law student in
her final year of undergraduate studies.

To the One I Love

I wish the world were made up of people like you.
For the sound of your laughter,
The warmth of your being,
And the touch of your hand
Urge me into the beauty of living.

Strengths

In the midst of a cold English winter
A small black face
wrapped tightly in woollen scarves
Plays in a school yard
Remembering
Laughing faces, warm breezes and strong straight
people.

What's New?

10.00pm
Night life begins.
It's after dark,
Can you hear the sirens
Of establishment hark?
The city girls are looking slick,
The men, suave, superficial,
The night weaves its little tricks.
Time to down the blues
Nothing really new.

11.00pm
Psychedelic lights, flash!
Another bum has a crash!
Can you feel the electric heat?
The walls reverberate
To the hypnotic beat.
Journey into fantasies
Drowning out realities.
Feeling a depression?
Got the blues?
Yeah, there is a recession,
So tell me, what's new?

Sandra Woods
Sandra Woods was born in Liverpool
in 1942 where she lives with her four
sons and eight grandchildren. She has
fostered sixty seven children of various
nationalities and is shortly to return to
college in preparation for a new career.

If Kids Ruled the World

The day my youngest started school
He was the only black kid there,
But the other kids didn't notice
Or really seem to care.
They laughed and played their little games
And he joined the football team,
He played so well they'd not have cared
If he'd been blue or green.
His fame must have spread, because one day
Whilst waiting for our sons
I joined the conversation
With several other mums.
They asked, "Well, which is David's mum?"
I said it was me.
One told me he was her son's best friend
And invited us for tea.
When at last the school let out
Our lads were running wild
I bent to tie the shoelace
Of that friendly mother's child.
She asked her son, "Which one is Dave?"
He pointed with his boat,
"That's him in the middle Mum,
In the light blue duffle coat."
She looked at me and staggered

As if she'd had a smack,
"Oh," she spluttered, "I didn't know
Your little boy was black."
She grabbed her son and scurried off
I felt a pang of sorrow,
I knew their lovely friendship
Would start to die tomorrow.
If only adults could be like kids,
There would be no racial rage
And we'd all live in a perfect world
No black, white, brown – just beige.